Supplementary V

C000040656

LANDS AND PEOPLES
IN ROMAN POETRY
THE ETHNOGRAPHICAL
TRADITION

RICHARD F. THOMAS

Associate Professor of the Classics
Harvard University

THE CAMBRIDGE PHILOLOGICAL SOCIETY
1982

ISBN 0 906014 03 4

DM

Theodore F. Thomas

. . . . .

omnis curae casusque levamen.

Printed by the Cambridge University Library

CONTENTS

ACKNOWLEDGEMENTS

This study began its life as a doctoral dissertation completed at The University of Michigan in 1977, and entitled *Ethnography and the Landscapes of Augustan Poetry*. It has since been completely reworked, and, as the present title suggests, the scope has also become somewhat broader. The chapters on Lucan and Tacitus in part serve to give focus to those on the Augustan poets, and, I trust, will be of interest in themselves.

For advice and suggestions I thank Professors W. V. Clausen and L. Koenen. Professor Z. Stewart read and commented thoroughly on the penultimate draft. I am also grateful to Professor E. J. Kennéy for editorial and other advice in the final stages. It remains to thank Professor D. O. Ross, who advised the original thesis, and whose help in that as in other matters has been invaluable.

Financial assistance from the Loeb Classical Library Foundation has helped to make this publication possible.

INTRODUCTION
THE TRADITION

With its seeds in the Homeric poems, and continuing into late Latin, the tradition of ethnographical writing is one of the most enduring in classical literature. Behind it there lies a function which provides the explanation for such endurance: by creating a formulaic literary genre to describe the features of other lands and the characteristics of their inhabitants, Greek ethnographical writers, and the Romans after them, were able to depict the diversity of mankind, and thereby to reach a fuller understanding of their own cultures and of their place in the world.

It will be useful to detail the form of ethnography at its most finished stage, then to give an account of the development of the tradition. All of this will be brief.[1] The term as it is understood in reference to Greek and Latin literature embraces both geographical and ethnological detail, and comprises (however brief the treatment) the following elements:[2]

1) Physical geography of the area
2) Climate
3) Agricultural produce, mineral resources, etc.
4) Origins and features of the inhabitants
5) Political, social and military organization

This is the barest outline, but it accommodates all the possible material of ethnographical studies.

The real beginning of the tradition was in the sixth century, as the data gathered from exploration and colonization were combined with a growing interest in scientific methodology. Obviously the movement was predominantly an Ionian one, and its central figure appears to have been Hecataeus of Miletus.[3] From the fragments (*FGH* 1 fr. 1-373) it is difficult to ascertain to what extent the various categories had been formulated; however, certain details survive, and in particular Hecataeus seems to have been interested in the *nomoi* of those lands with which he dealt.

With the fifth century came a realization of the artistic potential of the genre. The Egyptian and Scythian *logoi* in Herodotus (2.2-182; 4.5-82) are integral parts of his work, not merely gratuitous digressions: "Man is a part of the world as a whole and cannot be understood without inquiry into the world as it affects him".[4] However, it was not really until Hippocratic theories, particularly those contained in the treatise *Airs, Waters, Places*, were applied to ethnographical studies, that the true importance of the tradition was realized. Environment affects the health and, ultimately, the character of the inhabitants. Accordingly purely descriptive accounts of geographical features became central to ethnography, for the distinctions between people of different lands were seen as an outgrowth of, and directly attributable to, differences in environment. As a result (and the importance of this will emerge as we proceed) both diction and form became fixed, since divergence from the norm can only be expressed if there is standard, recognizable means of stating that norm.

The philosophers, particularly Plato and Theopompus, added a further dimension, incorporating ethical concepts into their ethnographical descriptions of mythical states. In these instances (e.g., Theopompus *ap.* Aelian *V.H.* 3.18 = *FGH* 115 fr. 75c – of Meropis; Plato *Critias* 114d1-121c4 – of Atlantis) each of the details is appropriate to a Utopian setting, but the format is ethnographical; thus descriptions of the mythical world are made credible through similarity to ethnographical descriptions of the real, attested world. Incidentally, the tradition of Utopian ethnography is as enduring as its "real" counterpart, and can be traced through to its most extreme point in Lucian's parodistic *True History*. This related tradition will play an important part in our study.[5]

The next step comes with the historians of Alexander, particularly Nearchus, Onesicratus and Cleitarchus. Ethnography had an obvious appeal, particularly if we accept the theory that these authors incorporated Alexander's universalism into their accounts of his achievements.[6] Also important at this point is the heightened interest in *thaumasia*, which, as we shall see, came to occupy an important position in ethnography.[7]

Posidonius seems to provide the main connection to Rome. "Panposidonianism" has rightly come under attack in the last half-century, but here a distinction must be made: it is Posidonius as *philosopher* whose influence has been overrated. Even those who have been in the forefront in correcting the false impression are in agreement that as a geographer and recorder of ethnographical data he holds a central position.[8] And Eduard Norden conclusively demonstrated that Posidonius was the single most important figure in the transmission of such material from Greek to Roman writers.[9] At the same time – and this must be left to the side for now – he appears to have introduced into the tradition elements of Stoicism.

The works of Caesar and Sallust stand as clear evidence that the Greek ethnographical tradition had, before the Augustan period, passed into the mainstream of Roman literature. The same form was adopted, and an equivalent diction, to be equally formulaic, came into being. It will be useful, again briefly,[10] to examine these two authors, and thereby to establish the Roman tradition. The models are Caesar's ethnography of Britain (*B.G.* 5.12-14) and Sallust's of Africa (*B.J.* 17-19), as well as what appear to be the remnants of similar studies from the *Histories* on Pontus (*Hist.* 3 fr. 61-80M), Sardinia and Corsica (*Hist.* 2 fr. 1-11M), Crete (*Hist.* 3 fr. 10-15), and the area around the Taurus range (*Hist.* 2 fr. 82-87).

A preliminary, important point. Norden, in showing that the title of Tacitus'

Germania as given by Niccolò Niccoli (*de origine et situ Germanorum*) is correct, collected the instances of the phrase *de situ* + genitive of the country or people under study, and convincingly proved that it was the standard title for Latin ethnographical works.[11] The earliest examples he cites are: *res postulare videtur Africae situm paucis exponere* (*B.J.* 17.1); *cum de situ Pontico* [*Sallustius*] *loquitur* (*Hist.* 3 fr. 71M); *cum praedixero positum insulae* (*Hist.* 2 fr. 1M). The phrase, then, acts as an ethnographical *sphragis*.

So much for preliminaries; under the first category (*situs*) the shape (*forma*) of the land is first given, particularly in cases where the shape is distinctive (e.g., of islands):

insula natura triquetra cuius unum latus est contra Galliam.
(Caes. *B.G.* 5.13.1)
Sardinia in Africo mari facie vestigii humani.
(Sall. *Hist.* 2 fr. 2M)
speciem efficit [Pontus] Scythici arcus.
(Sall. *Hist.* 3 fr. 63M)[12]

Together with the shape, the position of the land is invariably described with reference to the points of the compass (Caes. *B.G.* 5.13.1-2; Sall. *B.J.* 17.4; *Hist.* 2 fr. 2M). And lastly, further definition is provided by mention of major physical features, notably coastlines, seas, rivers and mountain ranges (Caes. *B.G.* 13.7; Sall. *B.J.* 17.4; *Hist.* 2 fr. 82, 84M; *Hist.* 3 fr. 10M).

Under the category of climate the Romans created a precise equivalent to Greek terminology. Climatic conditions in Greek ethnography were generally defined in relation to the ideal – ἀέρος εὐκρασία or κρᾶσις τῶν ὡρῶν – that is, a balance of mixture of the seasons, with no one season disproportionate to the others.[13] The Latin equivalent is *caeli temperatio/temperatura*,[14] and a variant of this in fact occurs in the first example of Roman ethnography:

loca sunt temperatiora quam in Gallia remissioribus frigoribus.
(Caes. *B.G.* 5.12.6)

Sallust also, although he does not use this actual term, includes the treatment of climate in his ethnographical passages (*B.J.* 17.5; *Hist.* 3 fr. 64-65M[15]).

Obviously there is a close relationship between this category and the third, agricultural produce and mineral resources. Countries are generally considered from the extent to which they permit pursuit of the three major agricultural activities: crops, trees (chiefly olives and vines) and livestock. So Sallust of Africa:

ager frugum fertilis, bonus pecori, arbori infecundus.
(*B.J.* 17.5)

Or, less completely, of the area around the Taurus: *frugum pabulique laetus ager* (*Hist.* 2 fr. 83M).[16] The importance of this tripartite division will become clearer as we continue. Also under this category, the extent to which a society is civilized can be indicated by its agricultural activities. Caesar stated of the Britons occupying the interior of the island (as opposed to the more civilized [*humanissimi*] coastal inhabitants):

> interiores plerique frumenta non serunt, sed lacte et carne vivunt pellibusque sunt vestiti.
>
> (*B.G.* 5.14.2)

Clearly the degree to which mineral resources are realized will have the same implications. So much for this category; other details can be found in both authors (Caes. *B.G.* 5.12.3-6; Sall. *Hist.* 3 fr. 12, 66M *vis piscium* – of Pontus[17]).

Little need be said, by way of preliminaries, of the origins and features of the inhabitants under study. It is of particular note that these passages, and especially those from the *Histories*, tend to emphasize both the mythical origins and movements of migration.[18]

For the writer of ethnography the final category is naturally the most important. The institutions of different societies are of interest intrinsically and for the light they throw on the ethnographer's own culture. Here it is the oddity which receives attention, for instance the fact that the Scythians are a nomadic race (*Scythae nomades tenent, quibus plaustra sedes sunt, Hist.* 3 fr. 76M).[19] And of even greater interest is moral oddity or aberration; for instance, Caesar on the habits of the Britons:

> uxores habent deni duodenique inter se communes et maxime fratres cum fratribus parentesque cum liberis. sed si qui sunt ex iis nati, eorum habentur liberi quo primum virgo quaeque deducta est.
>
> (*B.G.* 5.14.4-5)[20]

Here it is the difference from Roman customs which motivates the author's interest. It is in this category, too, that we most frequently find the *thaumasion*, a feature pervasive to such studies.

Something should be said of the general function of ethnography within Sallustian history. His particular interest in geographical material has been noted;[21] the nature of this interest is worth considering. Here Herodotean ethnography is relevant. In the *Jugurtha* Sallust first presents the moral theory which is to be the background of the monograph (1-4). Next comes biographical information on Jugurtha and a summary of his relations with Rome (5-16). Then the ethnography of Africa (17-19) immediately prefaces Sallust's treatment of the actual war. The description is by no means gratuitous (we should always be wary of the word "excursus" when dealing with this tradition); for action is to be understood in terms of both setting and participants. As R. M. Ogilvie notes on Livy's excursus on Gaul (5.33.4-35.3): "such digressions were inserted to heighten suspense and to focus attention on the drama which is about to unfold".[22] The same function can be detected in the ethnographies of the *Histories*. Sardinia (*Hist.* 2 fr. 1-11M) is important as the setting of Lepidus' last attempts at rebellion, and of his death. The Taurus area (*Hist.* 2 fr. 82-87M) warrants a description since here P. Servilius carried out raids against pirate strongholds. Crete (*Hist.* 3 fr. 10-15M) is the background of M. Antonius' defeat at the hands of the pirates. And, finally, the ethnography of Pontus (*Hist.* 3 fr. 61-80) – apparently the most extensive remaining description – is included as this is the arena for Lucullus in his final battles of the Third Mithridatic War.[23]

Although the survey has been brief, it is, for the purpose of this study, justifiable. First, the ground has been adequately covered by those concerned with the prose tradition. Moreover, our only concern for the moment is to establish that before the Augustan period[24] the diction, form and artistic potential of ethnographical writing had made the transition into Latin literature.

A final point needs to be made. Until the *Germania* of Tacitus there seems to have been no self-contained ethnographical study. Rather, what exist are universal histories or historical treatises, to which formally separable ethnographies were attached, normally serving to highlight historical events. Likewise, in philosophical works we find descriptive ethnographies (real or mythical), operating as *aetia* to more central topics. This versatility makes the tradition suitable for transposition from one genre to another. It was accessible to poets no less than to other writers.

This, then, is the background. We can now examine the poetry of Horace, Virgil and Lucan, and observe the extent to which, in the creation of their poetic landscapes, they drew from this tradition. What will result will be an evaluation of their poetic, cultural and political attitudes towards their own environments and their national experience. By way of a postscript, these views will subsequently be tested through a study of the tradition as it emerges in the works of its most able exponent, Tacitus.

Interpretation of poetry is seldom objective; however, much of the subjectivity with which we approach it can be eliminated if it is possible to identify the traditional elements employed, and to observe the poet's use of those elements. Where he can be shown to embellish, reject or alter detail demanded by tradition, interpretative judgement is justified. Ethnography is particularly fruitful in this respect, in that its fixity of language and form make it an objective criterion against which the poet's intentions can be evaluated. Of course, none of this will work unless it is possible to attribute to the poet a learning which would embrace so seemingly alien a tradition. Their familiarity with ethnography will become clear; but in any case, particularly with Virgil and Horace, such a learning is to be expected. Perhaps more than any poets in the history of Latin literature they were conscious of the literary traditions which were their heritage, and of the possibilities those traditions held for new application.

NOTES

1. The prose tradition has been well covered, and what follows is in part a summary. The seminal work is that of Trüdinger. This is supplemented and extended by Norden, *Die germanische Urgeschichte*. Schroeder's work is an extremely valuable study of the uniformity of various ethnographical *topoi*. Less satisfying, but useful in its exhaustive coverage of the writers in this tradition: K. E. Müller, *Geschichte der antiken Ethnographie und ethnologischen Theoriebildung* I, Stud. zur Kulturkunde 29 (1972). For a brief but clear exposition of the major works in the tradition, see J. G. C. Anderson, *Cornelii Taciti De Origine et Situ Germanorum* (Oxford 1938) xiii-xvi.

2. This scheme can be found in much the same form in Ogilvie and Richmond 164; see too E. Wolff, "Das geschichtliche Verstehen in Tacitus Germania", *Hermes* 69 (1934) 136.

3. See Trüdinger 8-14.

4. H. R. Immerwahr, *Form and Thought in Herodotus*, APhA Monographs 23 (1966) 315; also 312-323.

5. Perhaps still the best treatment of Utopian ethnography is that of E. Rohde, *Der griechische Roman und seine Vorläufer*, 3rd ed. (Leipzig 1914) 178-309.

6. W. W. Tarn, "Alexander, Cynics and Stoics", *AJP* 60 (1939) 41-70; the evidence is admittedly scant, but Tarn's case does seem plausible.

7. So Trüdinger 77-78; more generally, on the developments in the tradition at this time, see A. Dihle, "Zur Hellenistischen Ethnographie", *Grecs et Barbares*, Entretiens Fond. Hardt 8 (1961) 205-239.

8. J. F. Dobson, "The Posidonius Myth", *CQ* 12 (1918) 180, 195; also M. Laffranque, *Poseidonios d'Apamée* (Paris 1964) Ch. 5, "Poseidonios Géographe".

9. *Germ. Urgeschichte* Ch. 2, "Quellenkritisches zur Ethnographie europäischer Völker". Also Trüdinger 80-126, and J. J. Tierney, "The Celtic Ethnography of Posidonius", *Proc. Royal Irish Acad.* 60 Sect. C (1960) 189-275. The picture that emerges is that the major geographical writers after Posidonius (Strabo, Diodorus, Pompeius Trogus, Claudius Ptolemaeus, etc.) are predominantly indebted to him for ethnographical detail and theory.

10. For, again, studies of the subject in these authors are not lacking: Trüdinger 126-133; F. Beckman, *Geographie und Ethnographie in Caesars Bellum Gallicum* (Dortmund 1930); A. Klotz, "Geographie und Ethnographie in Caesars *Bellum Gallicum*", *RhM* 83 (1934) 66-96; specifically for ethnographical excursus in Sallust, R. Syme, *Sallust* (Berkeley and Los Angeles 1964) 153, 192-195.

11. *Germ. Urgeschichte* Anhang I 451-454.

12. The comparison to everyday objects seems to have been a commonplace of the tradition; cf. Ogilvie and Richmond on Tac. *Agr.* 10.3 - on the shape of Britain. Professor Kenney has pointed out to me that the description of Sicily at Lucr. 1. 716-721 is in this same tradition (cf. *triquetris*).

13. The concept, with this terminology, seems to appear first in the Hippocratic *Airs, Waters, Places* (12. 13-16), applied to the perfectly balanced climate of Asia Minor; thereafter it pervades ethnographical writings. Its importance will emerge as we proceed.

14. All of this has been known for some time; cf. J. Geffcken, "Saturnia Tellus", *Hermes* 27 (1892) 386; Norden, *Germ. Urgeschichte* 111 n. 1.

15. The main climatic feature of Pontus seems to have been its heavy fogs. Significantly, this same detail occurs in Menander's *Samia*, in a passage containing other ethnographical matter. Demeas and Niceratus have just returned to Athens from that area; the latter is relieved:

> ἐκεῖν᾽ ἐθαύμαζον μάλιστα, Δημέα,
> τῶν περὶ ἐκεῖνον τὸν τόπον· τὸν ἥλιον
> οὐκ ἦν ἰδεῖν ἐνίοτε παμπόλλου χρόνου·
> ἀὴρ παχύς τις, ὡς ἔοικ᾽, ἐπεσκότει.

(Sam. 106-109)

16. A. La Penna ("Sallustio, *Hist.* II 83M", *RFIC* 99 [1971] 61-62), on the basis of Claud. *de bell. Gild.* 509 (*dives ager frugum*), would re-assign this fragment to the beginning of the second book (*de situ Sardinae Corsicaeque*); although possible, this is not required, since such phraseology is commonplace to ethnography in general, not merely to descriptions of Sardinia.

17. Again, Menander seems to have known his ethnography; Niceratus, in disgust: Πόντος· παχεῖς γέροντες, ἰχθῦς ἄφθονοι... *Sam.* 98. Cf. A. W. Gomme and F. H. Sandbach, *Menander, A Commentary* (Oxford 1973) *ad loc.* for other references to Pontic fish (although none is specifically ethnographical).

18. Perhaps the best example is in Sallust, *B.J.* 18-19; he begins with the aboriginals of Africa, has Hercules pay a visit, and goes on to mention a number of other races (Medes, Persians, Armenians, Phoenicians, etc.). On the ubiquity of Hercules (and Odysseus) in ethnographical accounts, see Norden, *Germ. Urgeschichte* Ch. 3, "Herakles und Odysseus in Germanien".

19. Cf. also *Hist.* 3 fr. 85M, *genus hominum vagum*. This seems to have been a particularly appealing detail; it occurs in *Airs, Waters, Places* (18) as a feature of Scythian life, and is found elsewhere applied to various other races.

20. On the topical nature of polygamy in ethnographical studies, cf. Schroeder 21-24.

21. Cf. Syme, *Sallust* 192-195; generally on Sallust's geographical episodes, E. Tiffon, "Salluste et la géographie", *Littérature gréco-romaine et géographie historique*, Mélanges Dion, ed. R. Chevallier (Paris 1974) 151-160.

22. *A Commentary on Livy Books 1-5* (Oxford 1965) 701; Ogilvie points out that this is essentially a Hellenistic feature, but that it finds its beginnings in the practice of Herodotus and Thucydides.

23. It is perhaps not irrelevant to Sallust's artistic purposes that *agnomina* (derived from the area of their operations) accrued to two of these figures: Servilius Isauricus and Antonius Creticus. This is not, however, the case with Lucullus; see my note "L. Lucullus' Triumphal Agnomen", *AJAH* 2 (1977) 172.

24. Obviously subsequent Latin ethnography (e.g., that of Livy, Pompeius Trogus, Mela, Tacitus) will serve as a background throughout this study.

I. THE LANDSCAPES OF HORACE

Studies of Horace's poetic landscapes draw mainly from his lyric verse; the importance of the *Epistles* in particular seems to have been considered as minimal. For instance, the most recent book on the subject contains barely a mention of these poems.[1] This is, I think, explained by the guise in which Horace presented the *Epistles*; from the outset, in a way which should immediately arouse suspicion, he claimed to exclude the collection from the genre of poetry:

> nunc itaque et versus et cetera ludicra pono;
> quid verum atque decens, curo et rogo et omnis in hoc sum.
> (*Epist.* 1.1.10-11)[2]

So, with some exceptions,[3] critical focus has been on the philosophical stance of the poems ("Was Horace an Epicurean or a Stoic?"), or on the question of epistolary intent ("Were they written for the individuals addressed?"). The poetic merits of the *Epistles* have been somewhat obscured as a result.

The landscapes of the *Epistles* have fared little better than other elements. They have been used chiefly to support biographical criticism,[4] in the search for the locality of Horace's Sabine farm, its size, and so forth. The assumption with which we begin is that passages from the *Epistles*, no less than those from his lyric collections, are potentially both allusive and elaborately finished.

Horace's Sixteenth Epistle opens with a description of his farm, in response to a hypothetical question by Quinctius:

> Ne perconteris fundus meus, optime Quincti,
> arvo pascat erum an bacis opulentet olivae,
> pomisne an pratis an amicta vitibus ulmo,
> scribetur tibi forma loquaciter et situs agri.
> continui montes, ni dissocientur opaca   5
> valle, sed ut veniens dextrum latus aspiciat sol,
> laevum discedens curru fugiente vaporet.
> temperiem laudes. quid si rubicunda benigni
> corna vepres et pruna ferant? si quercus et ilex
> multa fruge pecus multa dominum iuvet umbra?   10
> dicas adductum propius frondere Tarentum.
> fons etiam rivo dare nomen idoneus, ut nec
> frigidior Thracam nec purior ambiat Hebrus,
> infirmo capiti fluit utilis, utilis alvo.

hae latebrae dulces, etiam, si credis, amoenae, 15
incolumem tibi me praestant Septembribus horis.
(*Epist.* 1.16.1-16)[5]

This conforms to the requirements of the ethnographical tradition. Horace indicates this with the very first words: *Ne perconteris*. B. Axelson has demonstrated the limited use of *percontor* in poetry (outside Plautus); apart from one instance in Propertius (2.22.23) it appears only in the *Satires* and *Epistles* of Horace.[6] In addition to being a prosaic word, it can have a specific sense closely related to our claims for the poem: it is, in fact, the Latin equivalent to ἱστορέω, as used by Greek geographers and historians.[7] Livy used it in this sense: *percunctatus regionis peritos de ascensu Haemi*, 40.21.3.[8] More importantly, Caesar had twice (*B.G.* 1.39.1; 5.13.4) used the noun *percontatio* in precisely the sense of the Herodotean ἱστορίη. The second instance, moreover, occurs in the ethnography of Britain, referring to enquiries made concerning the northern boundaries of that country: *nos nihil de eo percontationibus reperiebamus.*[9] This geographical sense is also reflected in Festus' epitome of Verrius Flaccus, where both derivations seem to have connections with exploration and the *periplus*:

ex nautico usu, quia conto pertentant, cognoscuntque navigantes aquae altitudinem...mihi ad falsum videtur: nam est illa percunctatio, quod is, qui curiose quid interrogat †percunctarisit†.
(Festus p. 236 Lindsay)[10]

So much, then, by way of introduction. Horace's choice of the word, in connection with possible enquiries about technical features of his farm (lines 2-3), may be influenced by the meaning it has in a geographical or ethnographical context. It remains to be seen whether such a reading is necessary.

The first category in Horace's description is the lay-out of the farm:

scribetur tibi forma loquaciter et situs agri.
continui montes, ni dissocientur opaca
valle, sed ut veniens dextrum latus aspiciat sol,
laevum discedens curru fugiente vaporet.
(4-7)

Scribetur ... loquaciter has caused some trouble, chiefly, of course, because the description is anything but *loquax* in the sense of "wordy". Pseudo-Acron comments at this point: *quod Graeci lalisti dicunt, non poetice, sed quasi prosa oratione et communi sermone ac simplicibus verbis* (*ad loc.*). Again the affinity with prose.

In fact, the language of line 4 may usefully be compared to that of Tacitus[11] in the introduction of his ethnography of Britain (*Agr.* 10.1-3):

Britanniae *situm* populosque multis *scriptoribus* memoratos ... referam ... *formam* totius Britanniae Livius veterum, Fabius Rusticus recentium *eloquentissimi* auctores oblongae scutulae vel bipenni adsimulavere.

The four main elements in Horace's introductory declaration (*scribetur, forma, loquaciter, situs*), together with a dependent genitive (*agri*) are all present in Tacitus' account. Most important, however, is the fact that Horace states that he will describe the *situs* of his farm (its shape – *forma* – being a part of this), which is uniformly the first category of ethnographical writing.

This leads to a further point. We have already referred to Norden's catalogue of titles of ethnographies giving the formula *de situ* + genitive.[12] Now in both of the manuscript traditions of the *Epistles* (probably derived from the edition of Valerius Probus), *Epistle* 1.16 is prefaced with the title *ad Quintium. de situ agri sui*. Why not *de forma*? And, for that matter, only one fifth of the poem is given to the description of the farm. In view of the pervasiveness of the phrase, the parallel can scarcely be accidental: it seems reasonable to assume that from a time not long after the writing of *Epistle* 1.16 the poem was acknowledged as having affinities to the ethnographical tradition.

With this introduction, then, Horace proceeds with his description: *continui montes, ni dissocientur opaca/valle*. The meaning seems to be that the farm is situated in a valley formed by a break in a circle of hills; compression hinders reconstruction. As M. J. McGann has noted: "Lines 5-14 are characterized by an extraordinary unwillingness to make statements of fact about the farm".[13] But this is the whole point; Horace is not concerned with giving a detailed description from which the reader will be able to reconstruct the farm's site and shape (although this has been done). Rather, his intent is to conform to the pattern of the tradition in which he is writing – each category must be covered, however briefly. As we saw with Sallustian ethnography, brevity is well established in the tradition.

Horace's use of *continuus* is perhaps of interest; before this instance, it appears only once with reference to physical features (Varro *ap.* Prob. Virg. *Ecl.* praef. [III.2 p. 326 Thilo]). Horace uses it only here. From this point it occurs frequently, being used to describe geographical features of an unbroken nature, and is found within ethnographical accounts.[14] It need not follow that Horace influenced its later usage, but the connection is of interest. In passing, it is worth noting that the word is in any case the Latin equivalent of συνεχής, which likewise occurs in such a setting (Herod. 4.22; Strabo 11.6.2).

The second part of this category conveys the aspect of the farm:

> sed ut veniens dextrum latus aspiciat sol,
> laevum discedens curru fugiente vaporet.

(6-7)

The rising sun touches the right-hand side of the valley; as it sets it hits the left side. The farm thus has a southerly exposure, the ideal aspect according to both Cato (*de agr.* 1.3) and Varro (*res rust.* 1.7.1).[15] These lines, moreover, conform to the requirements of the tradition, in that the *situs* is given in relation to the rising and setting of the sun.[16] Horace, then, by using such terms, effects a magnification of his environment, and at the same time suggests that it is ideal in its setting.

The next feature with which he deals is climate.[17] Typically Horatian compression may lead us to underestimate the full force of the sentence *temperiem laudes*. The meaning is clear: "You would praise its temperate climate". Yet the significance reaches beyond this. We have already mentioned that the concept present here is central in ethnographical treatments of climate. The primary expressions of an ideal climate were *temperatio* (Cic. *Verr.* 4.98) or *temperatura* (Varro *ap.* Non. 179.12); alternatively the participial adjective *temperatus* could be used (Caes. *B.G.* 5.12.6). The word *temperies* first appears in Horace's Epistle (the only instance of it in his works), and it is likely to have been coined by him as the only form which would be accommodated by the hexameter.

By way of digression, the importance of the word may be observed through its appearance in Augustan poetry. Virgil seems to have commented on the word (and possibly on the metrical inadequacies of existing substantives) when he paraphrased a passage from Eratosthenes (fr. 16 Powell), dealing with the five terrestrial zones (*Geo.* 1.231-258). For Virgil the most important lines are clearly those treating the two habitable zones of the centre:

δοιαὶ δ᾿ ἄλλαι ἔασιν ἐναντίαι ἀλλήλῃσι
μεσσηγὺς θέρεός τε καὶ ὑετίου κρυστάλλου,
ἄμφω εὔκρητοί τε καὶ ὄμπιον ἀλδήσκουσαι
καρπὸν Ἐλευσίνης Δημήτερος· ἐν δέ μιν ἄνδρες
ἀντίποδες ναίουσι.

(15-19)

Virgil, having closely described the climates of the uninhabitable zones, merely says of these temperate areas:

has inter mediamque duae mortalibus aegris
munere concessae divum.

(*Geo.* 1.237-238)

Where an equivalent is expected to Eratosthenes' εὔκρητοι, there is only silence. This expectation is clearly reflected in Servius Auctus:

DUAE MORTALIBUS AEGRIS: sicut dictum est, temperatae ex calido medio et frigidis extremis circulis.

Having described these zones, Virgil then proceeded to relate the uses to which a knowledge of this system can be put. Five times in twelve lines he used words with the root *temp-*, without including a variant of *tempero* (*intempesta* 247, *tempestates* 252, *tempusque* 253, *tempestivam* 256, *temporibusque* 258). Such a concentration with this poet can hardly be accidental. Virgil has artfully emphasized the element of *temperies*; the reader is supposed to note the omission (as it is noted in the Servian commentary), and in addition he is to observe Virgil's subsequent acknowledgement of that omission.

Ovid was also to adapt the lines of Eratosthenes, and he (with the advantage of Horace's *temperies*?) restored the appropriate term:

> totidem inter utrumque locavit,
> temperiemque dedit mixta cum frigore flamma.
> (*Met.* 1.50-51)

Ovid stressed the notion by adding a gloss: *mixta cum frigore flamma* (μείγνυμι/*misceo*, κεράννυμι/*tempero*).

After its appearance in the Sixteenth Epistle, the form *temperies* was frequently used, both in ethnographical contexts and in related areas, in the discussion of climatic perfection.[18] Tacitus, it should be noted, preferred it, employing it twice (*Ann.* 4.55.4; 4.67.2[19]); the "unpoetical" variants he never used. His complete avoidance of the term in his ethnographical works is perhaps due to its being such a commonplace.

So much for the development of the word. Now in ethnographical studies extremes of temperature – in either direction – result in deficiencies in the inhabitants. Diodorus has an extended discussion of this (3.34), and the idea is altogether traditional.[20] Thus the presence or absence of *temperies* is important; in claiming it for his environment (and it is peculiar to Horace's specific environment – *laudes*), Horace does more than merely suggest a balance between heat and cold. For implied in that balance is an environment which is totally at harmony and ideal, free from disease[21] and endowed with a natural and spontaneous fertility.[22]

Under the category of agricultural produce two passages are relevant:

> Ne perconteris fundus meus, optime Quincti,
> arvo pascat erum an bacis opulentet olivae,
> pomisne an pratis an amicta vitibus ulmo,
> scribetur ...
>   (1-4)

>   quid si rubicunda benigni
> corna vepres et pruna ferant? si quercus et ilex
> multa fruge pecus multa dominum iuvet umbra?
> dicas adductum propius frondere Tarentum.
>   (8-11)

The poem opens with an anticipation of Quinctius' question concerning the produce of the farm; does it have ploughland (*arvo*), olives (*bacis ... olivae*), fruit-trees (*pomisne*), pasture (*pratis*), or vines (*amicta vitibus ulmo*)? Now of the nine categories mentioned by Varro, the four omissions in Horace's poem are significant:

> secundus ubi hortus inriguus, tertius ubi salicta, ... septimus ubi caedua silva, ... nonus ubi glandaria silva.
>
> (*res rust.* 1.7.9)

These four are associated with small farming, whereas the five in Horace's poem have connections with large-scale agricultural activity. In fact, the five categories comprise the three general divisions of agronomy: crops, trees (including vines), and livestock. And as has been noted in the case of pre-Augustan ethnography, these three categories are the ones which consistently appear in discussions of the produce of various lands.[23] This continues to apply for subsequent writers in the tradition.[24] In particular, the degree to which each activity is pursued serves as an indicator of the cultural level of the society (cf. Strabo 4.5.2).

Horace, then, in the opening lines of the poem, used categories found in ethnographical works. Moreover, as comparison with the passage of Varro demonstrates, he appears to have deliberately suppressed those categories which would be appropriate to a small, private farm. The result, as in other parts of the description, is that the Sabine farm is magnified, as it is equated to a larger environment by means of ethnographical detail.

When Horace dealt with the actual produce of his farm (in the correct position, after *situs* and climate), he claimed a very different type of agricultural pursuit from that which Quinctius would have presumed to exist. In the place of conventional items there are cornel-berries (*corna*) and wild plums (*pruna*) – the poor man's olive.[25] In addition, the oak (*quercus*) and holm-oak (*ilex*) provide acorns for his herd (presumably pigs) and shade for Horace himself.

What is the significance of these lines? There is a suggestion of Horatian frugality in the description, but this is not in itself a sufficient explanation. Where an exposition of traditional products is expected, what appears seems a very poor substitute. Moreover, one can assume from elsewhere (*Sat.* 2.6.1-3) that Horace at the very least enjoyed the benefits of a vegetable garden. Here the implications are the reverse; conventional agriculture is minimal. L. Voit is, I think, correct in his claim that Horace has applied a feature of the golden age to his farm.[26] The oak-tree, spontaneously producing acorns as food, has associations with Dodona and with the birth of man in Arcadia.[27] Spontaneous growth also characterizes the other items. And, once again, there is an element of the *thaumasion* in Horace's claim: *quid si rubicunda benigni/ corna vepres et pruna ferant?* Brambles producing food. As in its climate, so in produce the farm shows signs of the marvellous.

Digression is again called for, and again the subject is Virgil. In lines 8-11 Horace referred directly to the closing lines of the "excursus" on the old man of Tarentum:

ille etiam seras in versum distulit ulmos
eduramque pirum et spinos iam pruna ferentis
iamque ministrantem platanum potantibus umbras.
                    (*Geo.* 4.144-146).

The dictional parallels are unmistakable; beyond this, the sequence is the same in both passages: from berries and fruit to larger trees administering shade. A further parallel exists; Virgil explicitly excluded from the old man's garden the three conventional agricultural pursuits:

nec fertilis illa iuvencis
nec pecori opportuna seges nec commoda Baccho.
                    (128-129)

Virgil's purposes will be the concern of the next chapter; for now it is sufficient to note that Horace followed him in also excluding these categories, after having suggested them in the opening lines of *Epistle* 1.16.

In the final two lines of his description Virgil concluded:

verum haec ipse equidem spatiis exclusus iniquis
praetereo atque aliis post me memoranda relinquo.
                    (147-148)

The *praeteritio* is, of course, common enough in Latin literature; purporting to pass over, it in fact emphasizes. This particular instance, especially with the second line, is unusually explicit, and all the more emphatic when considered with lines 116-117, which form the opening frame of the passage:

atque equidem, extremo ni iam sub fine laborum
vela traham et terris festinem advertere proram ....

The stress on delegation to a later author is also somewhat unusual. Certainly Columella took the lines to heart, introducing his tenth book (in hexameters) with the following:

isque [cultus hortorum], sicut instituteram, prosa oratione prioribus subnecteretur exordiis, nisi propositum meum expugnasset frequens postulatio tua, quae praecepit, ut poeticis numeris explerem Georgici carminis omissas partes, quas tamen et ipse Vergilius significaverat, posteris se memorandas relinquere.
                    (Colum. 10. *praef.* 3)

It is our suggestion, then, that Horace, the other poet of the Italian countryside, also heeded Virgil's call. This fact, moreover, elucidates Horace's statement at line 11:

dicas adductum propius frondere Tarentum.

He means Virgil's Tarentum; the claim is that his own farm possesses those same qualities which Virgil imputed to the plot of the old man. Without investigating those qualities at this time, a simple point should be noted: Virgil's passage is the central excursus from what has been recognized as an ethnographical description of the world of the bees.[28]

To summarize: in the opening lines of the poem Horace listed what would be the conventional areas of agricultural pursuit in an ethnographical study. In lines 8-11 the reader's expectations are then confounded by the introduction of items not normally found in such studies. The environment is hereby distinguished from highly civilized societies with the result, not that it is aligned with barbarous lands (which in prose ethnographies would be the result of such "deficiencies"), but rather that it is idealized. At the same time, Virgil's Tarentum is implicated.

Horace proceeds to the next feature of his farm:

> fons etiam rivo dare nomen idoneus, ut nec
> frigidior Thracam nec purior ambiat Hebrus,
> infirmo capiti fluit utilis, utilis alvo.
>
> (12-14)

Treatment of these lines has been predominantly biographical; perhaps inevitably, with varying degrees of caution, commentators since Pseudo-Acron have suggested that this could be the *fons Bandusiae* of *Odes* 3.13. Such views help little in understanding the poem.

The importance of the lines rests first in the phrase *rivo dare nomen idoneus*. Through it, Horace magnifies his spring by equating it to a river; then, by a massive hyperbole, he introduces the Thracian Hebrus: it is no cooler, nor any clearer than his own spring. In these lines he thus makes the description suit an ethnographical context; for rivers constitute an important part of that tradition. Herodotus gave them a special place,[29] and they are clearly important in that so often they define countries. In historical ethnography they assume an even greater importance, in that they serve as the natural boundaries which enforce harmony on man, and their being crossed often implies a transgression which leads to disastrous consequences. The examples are plentiful enough and hardly need mention.[30]

The use of *ambire* in line 13 is of interest. Horace has it with an impersonal subject only here. For elaboration, let us turn to Varro's theory on the word's etymology:

> amnis id flumen quod circuit aliquod; nam ab ambitu amnis.
>
> (*ling. lat.* 5.28)

The word, then has strong associations with rivers,[31] and is, in fact, frequently used in ethnographies to describe the course of rivers in relation to the countries through which they pass.[32] Horace claims: "My spring is as cool and pure as the Hebrus, which winds around Thrace". The diction has affinities to that of ethnography, and the allusion is to a country of the type dealt with in such works, and to one of its rivers, which would also be included in the study. Consider, for instance, Mela 2.16-17:

> His Thracia proxima est ... paucos amnis qui in pelagus evadunt, verum celeberrimos Hebrum et Neston et Strymona emittit.

In the quality claimed for this spring, once again the special character of Horace's environment is clear:

> infirmo capiti fluit utilis, utilis alvo.

This line has two main functions. The first lies in the anaphora, *utilis, utilis*, which prepares us for *incolumem ... me* (16), aiding the transition from correct environment to correct way of life, the main theme of the rest of the poem.[33] But more important for our purposes is the fact that the medical theory expressed in the line can be traced directly to *Airs, Waters, Places*, the treatise which so influenced ethnographical theory on the effects of environment on man. Elsewhere[34] there are indications that Horace was familiar with this work, and, in light of his artistic purposes in *Epistle* 1.16, direct influence seems plausible. The author of the work treats the effects of winds on water, and the resulting condition of the inhabitants. First, those areas sheltered from the north winds, and therefore having a brackish water-supply:

> τούς τε ἀνθρώπους τὰς κεφαλὰς ὑγρὰς ἔχειν καὶ φλεγματώδεας, τάς τε κοιλίας αὐτῶν πυκνὰ ἐκταράσσεσθαι ἀπὸ τῆς κεφαλῆς τοῦ φλέγματος ἐπικαταρρέοντος.
>
> (3)

And when the opposite conditions pertain:

> τοὺς δὲ ἀνθρώπους εὐτόνους τε καὶ σκελιφροὺς ἀνάγκη εἶναι, τούς τε πλείους τὰς κοιλίας ἀτεράμνους ἔχειν καὶ σκληρὰς τὰς κάτω, τὰς δὲ ἄνω εὐρωτέρας· χολώδεάς τε μᾶλλον ἢ φλεγματίας εἶναι. τὰς δὲ κεφαλὰς ὑγιηρὰς ἔχουσι καὶ σκληράς.
>
> (4)

The head and digestive tract are the areas most affected by the condition of the water.[35] So Horace, in an ethnography of his farm, claims that his spring has positive effects on precisely these two areas (*capiti ... alvo*). Incidentally, in the previous Epistle, when discussing the waters of Clusium, Horace had also dealt in terms of the effects on these areas (*qui caput et stomachum supponere fontibus audent/Clusinis*, 8-9).

So, in claiming this quality for his farm, Horace has in effect introduced the category concerning inhabitants, although, of course, this has been in the background throughout the description.

The account is now completed:

> hae latebrae dulces, etiam, si credis, amoenae,
> incolumem tibi me praestant Septembribus horis.
> (15-16)

Having established his farm as the ideal setting, Horace concludes by claiming for it *amoenitas*. The *locus amoenus* implicitly possesses great fertility,[36] often verging on the marvellous.[37] At the same time, there are suggestions of the secluded world of the poet; hence *latebrae*.[38] In a context clearly connected with the world of poetic creation Horace had already applied the word to his rural setting:

> Velox amoenum saepe Lucretilem
> mutat Lycaeo Faunus.
> (*Odes* 1.17.1-2)[39]

At this point the whole description can be more closely related to the ethnographical tradition. The farm's balanced climate, the unusual productivity, and the coolness and clarity of its health-giving spring are all to be seen as ethnographical *thaumasia*.[40] Accordingly, at the close of the description (15), Horace added the parenthesis, *si credis*. Far from expressing Horace's argumentative stance towards Quinctius,[41] it elucidates the whole description. For this phrase, or some variant of it (e.g., *si credere dignum est, si credere velis*), is regularly found in the company of ethnographical *thaumasia*,[42] and appears to have been attracted from such passages into straightforward and verifiable ethnography.[43] Thus the phrase explains the *amoenitas* of Horace's farm – a quality existing both as an ethnographical *thaumasion*, and as a natural phenomenon of the poet's environment.[44]

The tradition from which Horace drew in describing his farm should now be clear; the precise nature of his use of that tradition has already been suggested: the features are idealized, implying the same perfection as is found in Utopian ethnography. Another quality is present, however: the environment possesses features which elevate it as an ideal poetic setting. This can be clarified through observation of parallels between this poem and another major "country" epistle, 1.10.

1.10.15-21	1.16.8-13
est ubi plus tepeant hiemes,	temperiem laudes.
ubi gratior aura/leniat et	
rabiem Canis et momenta Leonis,/	
cum semel accepit Solem furi-	
bundus acutum?	
est ubi divellat somnos	si quercus et ilex/...
minus invida cura?	multa dominum iuvet umbra?

deterius Libycis olet aut	ut nec/frigidior Thracam
nitet herba lapillis?	nec purior ambiat Hebrus.

purior in vicis aqua tendit	fons etiam rivo dare nomen
rumpere plumbum/quam quae	idoneus, ut nec/frigidior
per pronum trepidat cum	Thracam nec purior ambiat
murmure rivum?	Hebrus.

The characteristics in both poems are the same, although choice of diction and form (together with the additional details) renders the account in the later epistle ethnographical. And in each of the parallels, the environment is established as poetically congenial.

In the first this is more explicit in the Tenth Epistle: Sirius, destructive of poetic inspiration and production, is powerless here, just as it was in *Odes* 1.17.17-19:

> hic in reducta valle Caniculae
> vitabis aestus et fide Teia
>   dices ...

Next, in both passages Horace has stressed the presence of shade, conducive to sleep (stated in 1.10, implicit in 1.16 – *iuvet ... umbra*). Shade, of course, is a feature of poetically ideal settings at least from Theocritus (1.15-23; 5.31-32, 48-49; 7.88-89), but, especially when accompanied by suggestions of sleep, the tradition of Callimachean and neoteric *Dichterweihe* assumes a special importance. Callimachus himself was transported in a dream to Helicon, where he was received by the Muses (*Anth. Pal.* 7.42),[45] and Horace, at the scene of his own initiation aligned himself specifically with this tradition (*me ... ludo fatigatumque somno, Odes* 3.4.9-11).[46] Virgil also used the motif; Silenus in the Sixth Eclogue (*pueri somno videre iacentem*, 14), and Proteus in the Fourth Georgic (*facile ut somno adgrediare iacentem*, 404) are both presented as sleeping, immediately prior to singing songs which are among the most important of Virgil's lines. Horace was eventually to state the matter explicitly:

> scriptorum chorus omnis amat nemus et fugit urbem,
> rite cliens Bacchi somno gaudentis et umbra.
>   (*Epist.* 2.2.77-78)

Somnus, and particularly the type associated with the country, and in antithesis to the city, is a prerequisite for the writing of poetry. Its presence in the two epistles holds the same implications.

Augustan poetry, and particularly that of Horace, began to express a pride in its own achievement where previously emulation of Greek themes and genres had been the more normal attitude.[47] This attitude, the plea for equality or even superiority of native Italian elements, seems to be reflected in the third parallel. The exotic and distant features of Libya and Thrace are in no way preferable to Italian simplicity.

Juvenal, for whom such exotic elements have been imported to Rome, ousting her pristine simplicity, reflects the very same plea, when, in the Third Satire, he writes of his meeting with Umbricius at the Porta Capena (which has been destroyed as a poetic environment – *eiectis Camenis*, 16):

> quanto praesentius esset
> numen aquis, viridi si margine cluderet undas
> herba nec ingenuum violarent marmora tofum.
>   (18-20)

The closeness to Horace's question (*deterius Libycis olet aut nitet herba lapillis?*) may be no coincidence.

Of the final parallel – cool, clear streams – little need be said. The claim for clarity (*purior*) in both poems clearly is a reference to the Callimachean metaphor found at the end of the Hymn to Apollo; the small, pure stream (καθαρή ... λιβάς, 110-111) is preferable to the large, muddied Euphrates. Horace was, of course, thoroughly familiar with this as a metaphor for poetic style (*cum flueret lutulentus, Sat.* 1.4.11; *at dixi fluere hunc lutulentum,* 1.10.50). The further development in the Tenth Epistle, however, does deserve mention; the lead pipes of Rome have replaced Callimachus' Euphrates:

> purior in vicis aqua tendit rumpere plumbum,
> quam quae per pronum trepidat cum murmure rivum?
>   (20-21)

So Horace achieves a harmony between the metaphor with its poetic significance, and the overall theme of the epistle: the supremacy of the country (and specifically of his poetic landscape) over the city. The full construct is to be recovered through a combined reading of both poems.

So much for the description of the farm. The movement of the Sixteenth Epistle changes at line 17, as Horace adopts an ethical stance, first giving advice against delusion (17-40), then posing and answering the question, *vir bonus est quis?* (40-79). What characterizes these lines is the *type* of philosophical stance assumed by Horace: "all these elements give the epistle a strong flavour of the Stoicism of ἀρετή, κατορθώματα and the σοφός and set it apart from the rest of the book, which expresses the less arduous ideals of *decorum, carpe diem, nil admirari* and *aequus animus*".[48] The connection between Stoicism and ethnography, and its implications for this poem, will be of concern later;[49] for now it is sufficient to note that from an ideal environment, presented in ethnographical terms (and thereby distinguished from all other settings – this is the function of such descriptions), Horace is able to present an ethically ideal programme. Also, of course, implicit in the description and stated at the outset of the second part of the epistle, is the contrast between the ideal country setting and the city, the negative analogue in *Epistle* 1.10, and here the seat of self-delusion:

iactamus iampridem omnis te Roma beatum:
sed vereor ne cui de te plus quam tibi credas.
                              (*Epist.* 1.16.18-19)

The mention of Rome, casual as it may seem, must evoke comparison with the
Sabine farm.

One detail from this second half deserves attention. The final image of the poem
is Horace's adaptation of Eur. *Bacchae* 492ff. Horace's chained Dionysus,
representing the *vir bonus et sapiens*, asks of his captor:

quid me perferre patique
indignum coges?
                                 (74-75)

This is more than a mere translation of Euripides' εἴφ' ὅ τι παθεῖν δεῖ (492). Again
in the Fifteenth Epistle (whose similarities to the Sixteenth have already been
noted), Horace states of his own ability to make do with inferior wine in the
country:

rure meo possum quidvis perferre patique.
                                  (1.15.17)

Exact verbal repetition is uncommon in Horace, and a connection seems to suggest
itself: Horace, in his ideal environment, is capable of enduring anything (even bad
wine); Dionysus, the *vir bonus*, will do the same (even to the point of death; *moriar*,
79).

Horace's irony at these points should not be allowed to obscure the importance
of the passages. Again the ethnographical tradition provides the explanation;
specifically, the concept of *patientia* within such studies. Endurance, or lack of it, is
related to environment in *Airs, Waters, Places*.[50] Norden has demonstrated that
this relationship was developed throughout the tradition, and finally applied to the
Germans – the focus of his study (*laboris atque operum non eadem patientia,
minimeque sitim aestumque tolerare, frigora atque inediam caelo solove
adsueverunt, Germ.* 4.3).[51] Sallust provides evidence that the notion was current in
pre-Augustan Latin ethnography; he says of the Libyans, living under a harsh
climate: *genus ... patiens laborum* (*B.J.* 17.6). Virgil applied the term to the last
inhabitants of the golden age: *et patiens operum exiguoque adsueta iuventus* (*Geo.*
2.472); also in the *Aeneid*, in a speech dense with ethnographical references,
Numanus Remulus claims of the early Latins: *et patiens operum parvoque adsueta
iuventus* (9.607).[52]

There is, in Horace's claim for *patientia*, an apparent contradiction; for,
according to ethnographical theory, it is the harsh climate, not the ideal one, which
induces this quality. The claim is to some extent ironical, as is clear from the nature
of his endurance in *Epistle* 1.15 – tolerance for poor wine. 'At the same time, the

reason may lie partly in his imposition of Stoic ethics (under which *patientia* is normally ascribed to the hardy and primitive[53]) on his idealized ethnography.

Horace did not mention his farm again. Through ethnographical form he elevated it as a separate environment, in contrast particularly to Rome and "civilized" Italy, as the only milieu in which the correct poetic and ethical pursuits could be carried out. To understand the broader importance of this, we must turn back to the darker days of the early Thirties and the Civil Wars.

Epode 16 is Horace's bleakest statement about the situation in this period; whereas *Epistle* 1.16[54] can be seen as a presentation of the Italian countryside in perfection, there is no such hope in this earlier poem. Not only is Rome headed for destruction (*suis et ipsa Roma viribus ruit*, 2); the countryside itself is in a state of reversion (*ferisque rursus occupabitur solum*, 10). What all Rome's foreign enemies could not accomplish, her own civil disorder is bringing about. Horace's solution, his answer to Virgil's rolling back of the years to another golden age, is to advocate migration to the *beatae insulae*. If Virgil's precedence in this matter is accepted,[55] then *Epode* 16 can be examined in terms of its own tradition, and as a strikingly original and unified piece of work.

The theme of migration serves as a unifying element to the whole poem; just as the Phocaeans sailed away to Corsica under the threat of Persian domination (Herod. 1.165ff.), so, Horace exhorts, should those who would seek an escape from the carnage desert their ravaged city (15-22). The Herodotean oath and *adynata* are expanded, so that the whole section spreads over 26 lines (15-40). Lines 41-66 (also 26 lines) deal with the land which lies beyond the Etruscan shores, the positive environment which is to take the place of Rome. It will be useful to examine the nature of this environment.

In the second half of the poem, Horace sustains the theme of migration, but the setting here is both poetical and historical. Within the tradition of descriptions of Utopian lands, the Isles of the Blessed have a distinct place.[56] Islands are by nature inaccessible, a fact which doubtless gives rise to the pervasive nature of this tradition. Plato's Atlantis (*Critias* 114d1 ff.),[57] Theopompus' Meropis (Aelian *V.H.* 3.18 = *FGH* 115 fr. 75c),[58] Hecataeus of Abdera's Hyperboreans (Diod. 2.47.1 ff. = *FGH* 264 fr. 7), Diodorus' island beyond the Straits of Gibraltar (5.19-20), and the southern νῆσος εὐδαίμων of the shadowy Iambulus (*ap.* 2.55.1 ff.)[59] all come within this tradition, and can be seen as examples of the desire to conceive of a society of perfection, beyond the reach of civilization, and therefore immune to its evils. Similar to these descriptions are those of the Elysian Fields; indeed, the two concepts can be directly equated: *quod secundum poetas in medio inferorum est suis felicitatibus plenum ... secundum philosophos elysium est insulae fortunatae, quas Sallustius ait inclitas esse Homeri carminibus* (Serv. *ad Aen.* 5.735). It is clearly just a matter of rationalization.[60]

Plato's passage and those in Diodorus in fact constitute formal ethnographical descriptions. And, from the remaining fragments, it seems legitimate to assume that

Theopompus' account of Meropis was a part of the same tradition.[61] As would be expected, in these instances the stress is very much on *thaumasia*; the terminology and form of ethnography, applied to mythical and idealized settings, lend to the accounts a higher degree of credibility.

Roman examples appear to be as formal, and they reflect the same element of imposed reality. It has been recognized that Plutarch's description of the Blessed Isles (*Sert.* 8) derives from an account of Sertorius' flight in Sallust's *Histories* (1 fr. 100M).[62] Moreover, Horace's description of the islands in *Epode* 16 has similarities to that of Plutarch. Now what appears in *Sertorius* 8 is a strictly formal ethnography: *situs*, produce, climate and the predominant attribute of the inhabitants (σχολάζοντα δῆμον). The whole account is appropriately idealized, with these elements appearing more in the nature of *thaumasia* as is the case in *Epistle* 1.16. What remains of Sallust's version? At first sight very little:

> quas duas insulas propinquas inter se et decem milia stadium a Gadibas sitas constabat suopte ingenio alimenta mortalibus gignere.
>
> (*Hist.* 1 fr. 100M)

In this fragment alone, two of the categories of ethnography occur – *situs* and produce, the latter standing as a *thaumasion* of the island.[63] It seems reasonable to assume that not only was Plutarch's account based on that of Sallust, but also that the passage in the *Histories* originally constituted a complete ethnographical description. Significantly, then, in Sallust's *Histories* there existed real, historical ethnographies (above, p. 2), as well as mythical or Utopian instances, instilled with veracity by adherence to the diction and form of the "real" tradition. Horace was working within a specific and unmistakable tradition, as Pseudo-Acron realized:

> Oceanus, in quo sunt insulae fortunatae, ad quos Sallustius in historia dicit victum voluisse ire Sertorium.
>
> (*ad Epod.* 16.41)[64]

What, then, are the details of Horace's description? Of particular importance will be the divergences from detail in the Fourth Eclogue. The first point is simple but vital; where Virgil dealt with a number of stages and a changing environment, Horace's setting is static. Again, this is necessitated by the tradition. Within this set environment Horace included only those features which are appropriate to the Blessed Isles. Thus Virgil's tame lions, suitable in a golden age setting, but having no place in the tradition of Utopian ethnography, are removed from the description and placed in the first half, among the Herodotean *adynata* (*credula nec ravos timeant armenta leones*, 33).

The agricultural features of the islands represent the conventional categories: crops (43), vines, olives and fruit-trees (44-46), honey (47)[65] and livestock (49-52). Each, moreover, is produced, or acts, spontaneously (*inarata*, 43; *imputata*, 44; *suamque ... ornat arborem*, 46; *ex ilice* [rather than from a hive], 47; *iniussae veniunt*, 49; *refertque tenta ... ubera*, 50). This spontaneity is, of course, a feature of the golden age, but it is also very much a part of Utopian ethnography (Hom. *Od.* 7.120-121; Plato *Critias* 114d8 ff. Theopomp. *ap.* Ael. *V.H.* 3.18; Sall. *Hist.* 1 fr. 100M; Plut. *Sert.* 8).[66] Often in Roman poetry these traditions tend to coalesce, and from the last lines of *Epode* 16 it is clear that Horace envisaged his ideal land as at least approximate to a golden age setting. It is noteworthy, however, that the spontaneity of production in this poem is in terms of modern agriculture, which does not exist, and is explicitly excluded from the golden age – that is what defines it as the golden age. Clearly two separate but similar traditions are at work here; they become merged to form one ideal environment.

At lines 47-48 Horace introduced a stream into his account (*montibus altis/levis crepante lympha desilit pede*), where there was none in Virgil's account. This is also appropriate to an ethnographical context. The suggestion, moreover, is of a clear stream, just as in Epistle 1.16 – this is the force of *lympha*, and it is also implied in *montibus altis*.

The next topic is the island's climate (53-56, 61-62).[67] Again, the primary point is that climatic harmony is presented as a *thaumasion* (*pluraque felices mirabimur*, 53), precisely the case with the *temperies* of the Sabine farm. In addition, the concept is made explicit in the Sixteenth Epode: *utrumque rege* temperante *caelitum*, 56. H. Reynen has fully treated the connection between *temperies* and absence of disease (61-62) in this poem.[68] Disease is the result of imbalance, and on these islands, as on Horace's farm, such imbalance does not exist. Reynen has also shown the relationship between *temperies* and fertility: lines 53-56 explain the success of the island's crops (43-48); lines 61-62 of her livestock (49-52).[69] While in *Epode* 16 the connection is made explicit, in *Epistle* 1.16 Horace merely stated *temperiem laudes*; we are intended to make the necessary assumptions concerning *temperies*, and to recognize the nature of the environment in which this balance exists.

Horace deals with the inhabitants of the islands in two sections; first those who will *not* be found there:

> non huc Argoo contendit remige pinus,
>   neque impudica Colchis intulit pedem;
> non huc Sidonii torserunt cornua nautae
>   laboriosa nec cohors Ulixei.
>
>   (57-60)

Although the terms are negative, this is all quite traditional. As noted in the Introduction (above, p. 4), the origins of a culture's population deal predominantly in terms of mythological wanderers (particularly Hercules and Odysseus) and waves of immigration. Here there are both: the ubiquitous Odysseus, prototype of the Ionian periplus (πολλῶν δ᾽ ἀνθρώπων ἴδεν ἄστεα καὶ νόον[70] ἔγνω), and the Phoenicians, colonizers par excellence. Indeed, if these figures were the inhabitants of the Blessed Isles, the passage would read precisely like a Sallustian ethnography. But, of course, they are not, for such groups must be excluded from Utopia if it is to remain pristine.[71] This was, in fact, precisely the fate of Iambulus and his companions, expelled from the Blessed Isles of the south for the sin of being civilized (ἐκβληθῆναι ἄκοντας, ὡς κακούργους καὶ πονηροῖς ἐθισμοῖς συντεθραμμένους, Diod. 2.60.1). No other crime is mentioned; being a part of the civilized world is sufficient.

Instead of these more "conventional" inhabitants, then, the islands will be peopled by a very different group, depicted in obvious contrast to those excluded:[72]

> Iuppiter illa piae secrevit litora genti,
>   ut inquinavit aere tempus aureum;
> aere, dehinc ferro duravit saecula, quorum
>   piis secunda vate me datur fuga.
>
> (63-66)

Pietas, in opposition not only to the *impietas* of those who spoil Utopian societies, but also to that of the age that has brought about Rome's downfall (*impia ... aetas*, 9), is the attribute necessary for admittance to the Blessed Isles. Virgil was to make the same distinction when dealing with the cognate environment of Elysium:

> "non me impia namque
> Tartara habent, tristes umbrae, sed amoena piorum
> concilia Elysiumque colo".
>
> (*Aen.* 5.733-735)

The *locus amoenus* is open only to the *pii*.

The points of contact between *Epode* 16 and *Epistle* 1.16 should be clear. The world of the first is based on an idealization of the ethnographical tradition; the "real" Italian countryside of the Sixteenth Epistle is presented in the form of an ethnographical study – with its features credible, but approximated to an ideal landscape. In the first poem, the public crisis of Rome[73] is to be resolved by migration to a world whose spontaneity and perfection set it in direct antithesis to Italy and Rome of the Civil Wars. By the time of *Epistle* 16, many of the features of that ideal world had been restored, not to Rome (and that point is emphasized in lines 18-19), but to the Italian countryside, and, significantly, to the poet's farm, a *locus amoenus* and the only correct ethical and poetic environment.

What motivates this development and how does it come about? Actium and the end of civil strife can of course be invoked, even Maecenas' gift of the Sabine farm. Yet such considerations can only be the background against which the poet conceives his ideas and builds his constructs. And, more specifically, we have suggested that in this matter it is a private Italian world, not the world of Rome, which finds redemption. The development is essentially a poetic rather than an historical one.

Again, the final four lines of *Epode* 16:

Iuppiter illa piae ecrevit litora genti,
    ut inquinavit aere tempus aureum;
aere, dehinc ferro duravit saecula quorum
    piis secunda vate me datur fuga.
(63-66)

J. K. Newman notes of the last line: "Whatever the exact significance of the whole epode XVI, ... the use of *vates* in this context, political and yet with definite allusion to the Eclogues, shows that Horace had understood what Virgil meant (when using *vates* in the *Eclogues*)".[74] The substitution of *vates* for *poeta*, like that of *Camenae*,[75] is crucial for an understanding of the early poetry of Virgil and Horace. The *vates* holds a special position as prophet-poet, a position which, for Horace, reaches its most sublime in the Roman Odes, particularly in 3.4.[76] In the final line of the Sixteenth Epode, in terms which he was yet to develop fully (the role is not yet Pindaric in the sense of *Odes* 3.4 – a natural consequence of the still uncertain years between 40 and 38, and of Horace's relatively humble position at this time), he assumed towards Italy and Rome this role of prophet-poet. As such, he recommended evacuation of a devastated Rome and migration to a world which, within the tradition which has been indicated, was of his own creation. Through the *Odes* the obvious fiction of such a stance was removed, as the Italian landscape, and particularly Horace's own environment, came into its own.

The opening of *Odes* 1.17 depicts a setting that is solidly Italian:

velox amoenum saepe Lucretilem
    mutat Lycaeo Faunus.
(1-2)

Pan, with the Italian title Faunus, deserts Arcadia for the (presumably)[77] Sabine mountain, Lucretilis; in fact, he does so often.[78] The epithet *amoenum* will not go unnoticed. Just as the Sabine mountain replaces the usual Arcadia, so Pan becomes Faunus, with all the connotations of early Latin rusticity attending the name;[79] his functions are those of the Greek god, but Horace is not merely translating at this point. The effect of Faunus' visits is that Horace's farm comes to display precisely the same harmony detected in *Epode* 16 and *Epistle* 1.16:

    et igneam
defendit aestatem capellis
    usque meis pluviosque ventos.
(2-4)

Temperies again, with the same suggestion that disease is thereby kept from the poet's goats. This notion finds its corollary in the second half of the poem, where the farm's secluded valley wards of the heat of the Dog-Star, thus permitting Tyndaris' poetic activity to proceed unhindered:

> hic in reducta valle Caniculae
> vitabis aestus et fide Teia
>   dices laborantis in uno
>   Penelopen vitreamque Circen.
>   (17-20)[80]

Here, more than anywhere else, Horace is at work creating of his Sabine farm a poetically congenial environment. It is characterized by *temperies*, the motif for the harmonious environment which allows poetic creation. Where Jupiter provided that harmony elsewhere in *Epode* 16, here Faunus, a deity possessing associations with purely Italian poetry, creates it in the setting of Horace's own farm. At the same time Faunus wards off snakes and wolves (8-9), whose absence the very environment of the Sixteenth Epode ensured. And so, in this Italian setting, there occur traces of the golden age, impossible in the *Epodes*,[81] but divinely introduced in the *Odes*, and to exist unaided in the Sixteenth Epistle.

Horace further elaborated the reasons for the protection of his environment:

> di me tuentur, dis pietas mea
> et musa cordi est.
>   (*Odes* 1.17.13-14)

The poet's *pietas* and his *musa* are responsible for his protection; precisely the combination at the end of *Epode* 16. Newman has demonstrated the religious element inherent in the term *vates*.[82] It is Horace's position as *vates* which allows him to claim such *pietas*, and which brings about the special quality of his environment.

Elsewhere, at the setting of Horace's poetic initiation (*Odes* 3.4), again within a markedly emphasized Italian landscape,[83] and with the same element of divine protection (17-18), Horace was to stress the combination of *pietas* and *amoenitas*. The reminiscence of his own Blessed Isles and of Virgil's Elysium is striking:

> audire et videor pios
> errare per lucos, amoenae
>   quos et aquae subeunt et aurae.
>   (6-8)[84]

The last point of transition is *Odes* 2.6. After an address to Septimius, Horace prays that he may end his days in Tibur; if this is not possible, "Let Tarentum be my resting-place". The description of Tarentum then follows:

> ille terrarum mihi praeter omnis
> angulus ridet, ubi non Hymetto
> mella decedunt viridique certat
>   baca Venafro,

ver ubi longum tepidasque praebet
Iuppiter brumas, et amicus Aulon
fertili Baccho minimum Falernis
  invidet uvis.

ille te mecum locus et beatae
postulant arces; ibi tu calentem
debita sparges lacrima favillam
  vatis amici.

(13-24)

A harmonious climate, and produce equal to the best in antiquity.[85] In an Italian landscape, whose harmony and fertility come about through the poet's position as *vates*, his ashes will find their rest. Specifically, the blessed heights (*beatae ... arces*)[86] of Tarentum are the setting for this perfection.

The ethnographical description in *Epistle* 1.16 represents Horace's acknowledgement of the process we have traced. The Sabine farm and Tarentum stand as ideal landscapes, the product of poetic art. Through ethnography Horace acts as a virtual commentator on the poetic process which occurs between *Epode* 16 and the epistle; the ethnographical Utopia, with its overtones of the golden age, to which Horace claimed he could transport the pious through the power of poetry, is eventually restored to Italy through that poetry.

The prominence of Tarentum appears to be indebted to Virgil's lines on the old man in the Fourth Georgic (above, pp. 13-15); the next step will be an examination of Virgil's use of the tradition.

NOTES

1. I. Troxler-Keller, *Die Dichterlandschaft des Horaz* (Heidelberg 1964); also E. A. Schmidt, "Das horazische Sabinum als Dichterlandschaft", *Antike und Abendland* 23 (1977) 97-112.

2. The claim is artfully supported by the monstrous and unpoetic accumulation of elision in the second line.

3. Particularly E. Garn, *Odenelemente im 1. Epistelbuch des Horaz* (diss. [microfilm] Freiburg i. Br. 1954); C. Becker, *Das Spätwerk des Horaz* (Göttingen 1963); M. J. McGann, *Studies in Horace's First Book of Epistles*, Collection Latomus 100 (1969).

4. E.g., G. Lugli, "La villa sabina d'Orazio", *MAAL* 31 (1926) 457-598; here the epistles are used to recover the setting of Horace's farm. Also P. Brind' amour, "Paulum silvae super his foret", *REA* 74 (1972) 86-93.

5. This text is in essence that of the OCT; for the variant *si* at line 5, with a comma following *vaporet* (7), see O. Keller, *Epilegomena zu Horaz*, Dritter Teil (Leipzig 1880 [repr. Hildesheim 1976]) 661-662.

6. *Unpoetische Wörter, Ein Beitrag zur Kenntnis der lateinischen Dichtersprache*, Skrifter Utgivna av Vetenskaps-Societeten i Lund 29 (1945) 65; also H. Tränkle, *Die Sprachkunst des Properz und die Tradition der lateinischen Dichtersprache*, Hermes Einzelschriften 15 (1960) 135.

7. That ἱστορίη consisted mainly of personal enquiry can be assumed from Herod. 2.99, μέχρι μὲν τούτου ὄψις τε ἐμὴ καὶ γνώμη καὶ ἱστορίη ταῦτα λέγουσά ἐστι, τὸ δὲ ἀπὸ τοῦδε Αἰγυπτίους ἔρχομαι λόγους ἐρέων. Generally, on the importance of this in ethnography, see F. Jacoby, "Herodotus", *RE* Suppl. 2.205 ff.

8. Also Livy 44.35.10.

9. Norden (*Germ. Urgeschichte* 80, n. 1) and A. Klotz ("Geographie und Ethnographie in Caesars *Bellum Gallicum*", *RhM* 83 [1934] 72, n. 1) treating the first of these references, debate the practical problems of conducting such *percontatio*; they do not deal with the technical nature of the term.

10. Cf. also, for Paulus' summary, p. 237 Lindsay.

11. For now, Tacitean ethnography will be treated only as it is relevant to poetic versions; chapter VI will examine it for its own sake, and as a check against which the present views may be tested.

12. Above, Introduction, p. 2.

13. "The Sixteenth Epistle of Horace", *CQ n.s.* 10 (1960) 206; in comparing this description to others in Horace's works, McGann appears to see this taciturnity as a deficiency.

14. E.g., Trogus 36.3.2; Mela 1.117; 2.66, 85; Tac. *Agr.* 10.5; *Germ.* 43.3. Similar is Livy 9.2.7.

15. Varro elsewhere (1.12.1) claims that the eastern aspect is superior; P. Brind' amour believes this is the situation for Horace's farm: "une vallée allongée du nord au sud qui fait que la villa d'Horace est orientée vers l'est comme le prescrivait Varron" (above, n. 4, 91). But the lines themselves suggest rather than the villa is facing *down* the valley, i.e. to the south. Moreover, if we would invoke external evidence, this is the situation of the commonly accepted site, the valley dominated by the town of Vicovaro; see G. Lugli (above, n. 4). For the correct view, Kiessling-Heinze, p. 136; W. Wili, *Horaz und die augusteische Kultur* (Basel 1948) 40.

16. To the pre-Augustan examples given in the introduction (p. 3) may be added: Mela 3.16, 25; Pliny, *N.H.* 4.58, 114; 6.82; Tac. *Agr.* 10.2; *Germ.* 1.2.

17. Horace does not formally treat the category dealing with inhabitants, for obvious reasons. He does, however, obliquely do so at a later point, and he is at pains to place himself in the environment throughout the description (*fundus meus*, 1; *pascat erum*, 2; *multa dominum iuvet umbra*, 10; *incolumem ... me*, 16).

18. Ovid, *Met.* 1.430; 15.211; *Pont.* 2.7.71; Curt. 4.7.17; 9.1.11; Ammian. 23.46; Pliny, *N.H.* 3.41; 37.201.

19. See below, ch. VI, p. 127.

20. The incorporation of this theory into ethnographical studies seems to have been particularly a feature of Hellenistic studies; see A. Dihle, "Zur Hellenistischen Ethnographie", 215-217.

21. This notion, as it appears in *Epode* 16, is examined by H. Reynen, "Klima und Krankheit auf den Inseln der Seligen", *Gymnasium Beihefte* 4 (1964) 99; it will be more prominent when we come to deal with that poem.

22. On this connection in descriptions of Utopian societies, see Schroeder 41-44; also Reynen, "Klima und Krankheit", 99.

23. Above, Introduction, p. 3.

24. Trogus 2.1.11-12; 44.1.5-7; Tac. *Agr.* 12.5; *Germ.* 5.1; Ammian. 23.6.29-30; 23.6.45; 23.6.65.

25. Cf. Columella 12.10; Kiessling-Heinze on *Epist.* 1.16.9.

26. "Das Sabinum im 16. Brief des Horaz", *Gymnasium* 82 (1975) 414.

27. Olck, "Eiche", *RE* 5.2027; see 2030 for the fruit of the φηγός, introduced by Pelasgus (Paus. 8.1.5); also Voit 414-425, although I cannot agree with his conclusion, that in claiming such produce Horace has ironic intent.

28. So H. Dahlmann, *Der Bienenstaat in Vergils Georgica*, Akad. der Wiss. und der Lit. Mainz, Abhand. Geistes- und Sozialwiss. Klasse 10 (1954); this will be the focus of chapter 3.

29. Consider, for example, the position he gave to the Nile in his Egyptian ethnography (2.10-34), although, in that it is the most prominent feature of that country, this instance is somewhat out of proportion.

30. E.g., the Halys, Asopus, Araxes; the Bosporus appears in much the same light. See Trüdinger 21; also H. Immerwahr, *Form and Thought in Herodotus*, APA Monographs 23 (1966) 96-98; *passim*.

31. Virgil, typically, seems to have glossed the word: *moenia.../quae rapidus flammis ambit torrentibus amnis, Aen.* 6.549-550; see Norden *ad loc.*

32. Sallust *Hist.* 4 fr. 77M; Mela 2.27 (*ambitus*); Pliny *N.H.* 2.242; 4.40; 4.84; Tac. *Agr.* 10.6; *Germ.* 1.1; *Hist.* 4.79.3; Ammian. 14.8.10.

33. On the division of the poem, see E. Garn (above, n. 3) 67; M. J. McGann (above, n. 13) 208.

34. H. Reynen ("Klima und Krankheit", 98) tentatively suggested this in connecting the tradition of the climatically perfect Asia Minor (as it appears in *Airs, Waters, Places*) with that of the Blessed Isles in *Epode* 16; his qualification is perhaps unnecessarily cautious: "wenn auch kaum an eine direkte Benutzung von Hipp. aër. durch Horaz zu denken ist". For Virgil certainly knew of and applied the work; here see I. Borzsák, "Von Hippokrates bis Vergil", in *Vergiliana*, ed. H. Bardon and R. Verdière (Leiden 1971) 41-55.

35. See also 7.84 ff.; 9.22 ff. for effects on the κοιλίαι alone.

36. *CGL* 2.443.20, σύμφυτον, τὰ πολλὰ φυτὰ ἔχον; 5.265.6, *fertile, iucundum;* 4.308.45, *fertile, iocundum, fructuosum, uberum.*

37. E.g., as used by Virgil on Elysium (*Aen.* 5.734), or Valerius Maximus on Asia (4.8.4).

38. In view of the farm's other golden age features, it is possible that Horace intended, through *latebrae*, a reference to the supposed etymology of Latium, namely as the final hiding-place of Saturn: *Saturnus... arma Iovis fugiens et regnis exul ademptis/ ... Latiumque vocari/maluit, his quoniam* latuisset *tutus in oris./aurea quae perhibent illo sub rege fuere/saecula* (Virg. *Aen.* 8. 319-325); for the observation on Virgil's lines, see D. O. Ross, *Backgrounds to Augustan Poetry, Gallus, Elegy and Rome* (Cambridge 1975) 157, n. 4.

39. For this, see Steele Commager, *The Odes of Horace* (New Haven 1962) 348-352; also P. Pucci, "Horace's Banquet in *Odes* 1.17", *TAPhA* 105 (1975) 260. G. Schönbeck (*Der locus amoenus von Homer bis Horaz* [diss. Heidelberg 1962] 155-166) has demonstrated the importance of *Epistle* 1.16 as presenting an idealized *locus amoenus* imposed on a real landscape; his concern, however, is not with ethnography, which is precisely the means by which the reality is heightened.

40. Cf. Introduction, n. 7.

41. This is the view of M. J. McGann (above, n. 13) 206.

42. Pliny *N.H.* 2.205; 3.57; 9.38; 10.187; 28.102. Also with aetiological detail, which requires the same lapse of credibility: Virg. *Geo.* 3.391; *Aen.* 6.173; Ovid *Met.* 3.311; *Pont.* 1.8.13; *Aetna* 173; Sil. Ital. 3.425; Mela 2.3. [Cf. T. C. W. Stinton, *PCPS* 22 (1976) 60-89 (*Ed.*)]

43. Mela 1.23; Curtius 7.7.3; 9.1.24; Pliny *N.H.* 4.89; 5.132; Lucan 9.411-412; Tac. *Germ.* 40.5.

44. It is perhaps relevant that in *Epistle* 1.15, Horace, after questioning Vala about the weather, inhabitants, roads and produce around Velia and Salernum, concluded: *scribere te nobis tibi nos accredere par est* (25). Here Vala is to act as ethnographer (*scribere*), and Horace will accept the information (*accredere*); in *Epistle* 1.16 Horace is the author (*scribetur*), and, in spite of the marvellous nature of the information, Quinctius is to believe him (*si credis*).

45. Cf. also *Aet.* 1 fr. 2 and Pfeiffer *ad loc.* For the claim that the anonymous epigram reflects the diction of a Callimachean original, see Ross, *Backgrounds* 150.

46. See Ross, *Backgrounds* 149-150 for the debt to Callimachus in these lines.

47. For Horace particularly, this is evident in the substitution of Italian for Greek settings in programmatic passages; so Ross, *Backgrounds* 144-145.

48. So M. J. McGann (above, n. 3) 75.

49. See below, chapters 5 and 6.

50. Particularly ch. 12, where an easy environment leads to a lack of endurance in the inhabitants, and subsequently to a preoccupation with the pursuit of pleasure. Also ch. 15 for this as a quality of the people of Phasis.

51. *Die germanische Urgeschichte* 54; also 111. Tacitus' northern Germans, as well as those of Vitruvius (6.1.9), are sluggish on account of the extreme cold; Norden has shown that Posidonius' modification of Hippocratic theory, and Varro's application of such theory in his *laudes Italiae* (*Res Antiquae* 11), form the basis of Vitruvius' account.

II. FAILURE AND SUCCESS IN THE *GEORGICS*

"By and large I think it is fair to say that this great poem has been admired rather than understood". So one critic of the *Georgics* in an appendix to his own work on Virgil.[1] What chiefly seems to confound comprehensive explanation of the work is its defiance of attempts to impose any satisfactory unity upon it. In treating all parts of the poem with equal emphasis, critics are compelled to omit development of much which is significant; for it cannot be denied that some portions of the *Georgics* are on a higher literary level than others. And yet, as E. Burck has rightly argued,[2] by separating the poem into two parts – one technical and one more elevated or poetical – the critic damages the fabric of the work, and at the same time creates, or perpetuates, a familiar fallacy, namely that the didactic stance of the *Georgics* is much more than a fiction. This further has the effect of imposing on the non-technical sections of the poem the status of digression or excursus.

In treating the tradition of ethnographical writing as it appears in the *Georgics*, I will be at variance with the critical methodology forwarded by Burck, and to that extent this chapter and the next do not present themselves as a complete interpretation of the entire work. Nevertheless, such an approach is justified. For while Klingner is undoubtedly correct in claiming that the *Georgics* (unlike a "real" didactic poem, such as the *De rerum natura*) is so much more than the sum of its parts,[3] it is equally the case that no understanding of the whole will emerge without a realization of the significance of the parts. This seems particularly true of those sections which can be shown to be indebted to the ethnographical tradition. It will become clear that this tradition is Virgil's main source in his depictions of landscapes in the *Georgics*; only through an understanding of this source and through subsequent observation of the purposes to which Virgil put it will there emerge a full picture of his attitudes towards the various environments and their inhabitants in the poem.

First, on a broad, compositional level, the influence of the tradition on the *Georgics* is apparent. In ethnographical treatises, as has been demonstrated (above, pp. 3, 13), crops, trees and livestock are the three sub-divisions of the category, agricultural produce. Virgil, in the first three books of the poem, follows this same division. From the technical standpoint,[4] as well as the poetic one,[5] the treatment of the bees in *Georgics* 4 is separable. In fact, Virgil confirms this separation when, in concluding the work, he writes:

> haec super arvorum cultu pecorumque canebam
> et super arboribus, Caesar dum ...
>
> (4.559-560)[6]

Only the subjects of the first three books are included. Aristaeus makes the same omission in his complaint to Cyrene (*quin age et ipsa manu felicis erue silvas,/fer stabulis inimicum ignem atque interfice messis,/ure sata et validam in vitis molire bipennem,/tanta meae si te ceperunt taedia laudis*, 3.329-332).

As far as we know, Virgil's arrangement is not accounted for by the agronomical tradition. Nicander of Colophon may have provided him with a title, but is responsible for nothing in terms of arrangement; his work was in two books (Athen. 3.126b 5-7), and none of the surviving fragments has any sure connection with Virgil's poem.[7] Nor does Varro's treatise provide a compositional model; he divided his work into three books, dealing respectively with agriculture proper, domestic livestock, and smaller animals (birds, fish, bees, etc.). E. de St. Denis[8] sees the impulse for Virgil's arrangement in a sentence from Cicero's *De senectute* (*nec vero segetibus solum et pratis et vineis et arbustis res rusticae laetae sunt, sed hortis etiam et pomariis, tum pecudum pastu, apium examinibus, florum omnium varietate*, 54). The suggestion is *a priori* implausible; Cicero is hardly a likely source for Virgil. In addition, the categories in the *De senectute* are looser than those of Virgil; indeed, some do not even appear in the *Georgics* except in passing (e.g. *horti, pomaria, flores*).

The single area in which the three categories of the first three books consistently appear is in ethnographical writings.[9] And, even more significantly, all four categories of the *Georgics* occur under the heading of agricultural produce in Horace's *beatae insulae* (*Epode* 16. 43-50), a setting which, as we saw in the last chapter, is heavily influenced by this same tradition. In the broad fabric of the *Georgics*, then, ethnographical theory seems to be operative.

There is a further point. *Georgics* 4, although not treating a mandatory part of this ethnographical category, assumes in this study a major importance, in that Virgil consciously presented the world of the bees in the language of an ethnographical study.[10] This will be the subject of the next chapter; for now it is sufficient to note the compositional balance which results from this arrangement.

The focus will be primarily on three passages: the *laudes Italiae* (2.136-176), the 'excursus' on Libya[11] and Scythia (3.339-383), and the description of the old man of Tarentum and his plot (4.116-148). The general structural similarities among these sequences, as well as their formal dependence on the ethnographical tradition, can be seen from the following chart:

CATEGORY	LAUDES ITALIAE 2.136-176	SCYTHIA 3.349-383	TARENTUM 4.125-146
SITUS	136-9: Italy (line 138) introduced in contrast to other lands	349-51: at non qua Scythiae gentes Maeotiaque unda, turbidus et torquens flaventis Hister harenas, etc.	125-7: namque sub Oebaliae memini me turribus arcis, qua niger umectat flaventia culta Galaesus, etc.
PRODUCE	140-8: haec loca non ... sed gravidae fruges et Bacchi Massicus umor implevere; tenent oleae armentaque laeta. hinc, etc.	352-3: illic clausa tenent armenta, neque ullae aut herbae campo apparent aut arbore frondes; sed iacet, etc.	127-33: pauca relicti iugera ruris erant, nec fertilis illa iuvencis nec pecori opportuna seges nec commoda Baccho. hic rarum tamen, etc.
CLIMATE	149: hic ver adsiduum atque alienis mensibus aestas	354-9: sed iacet aggeribus niveis informis ... semper hiems, semper spirantes frigora Cauri	134-43: primus vere ... cum tristis hiems ... aestatem seram ... autumno
GENS	167-72: haec gens acre virum, etc.	376-83: talis ... gens effrena virum, etc.	127: Corycium ... senem (throughout in his activities; cf. Chapter I, n. 17)
THAUMASIA AND SOCIAL	150-66: *biferitas*, no lions, etc., artificial lakes, gold in rivers, warlike nature of inhabitants	360-80: effects of cold, hunting, cave-dwelling, beer-drinking, etc.	134-46: activities and self-sufficiency of old man
SOCIAL FEATURES	ETHNOGRAPHICAL PARALLELS IN VIRGIL'S *GEORGICS*		

Each of the environments is presented through the same form, and with parallel terminology. Further parallels and contrasts are created, moreover, by clear similarities of diction. Under the first category, the *situs* of Scythia and that of the old man's plot are described in what appears to be a deliberately parallel manner:

> at non qua Scythiae gentes Maeotiaque unda,
> turbidus et torquens flaventis Hister harenas ...
> (3.349-350)
> qua niger umectat flaventia culta Galaesus ...
> (4.126)

Both are defined by their rivers, a familiar ethnographical practice. In the second category, the pattern is the same for all three settings; one type of produce is presented in negative terms, with the actual situation stated by means of an adversative conjunction (*haec loca* non ... nec ... sed *gravidae fruges* ... 2.140-144; *illic clausa tenent stabulis armenta*, neque ... aut ... aut ..., sed *iacet aggeribus niveis informis et alto terra gelu late*, 3.352-355; nec *fertilis* ... nec ... *opportuna* ... nec *commoda* ... *hic* ... tamen ... 4.128-130). In each case, moreover, the issue is the presence or absence of the three traditional components of ethnographical agronomy. The climatic conditions of each setting are also presented in parallel terms:

> hic ver adsiduum atque alienis mensibus aestas.
> (2.149)
> semper hiems, semper spirantes frigora Cauri.
> (3.356)
> vere ... tristis hiems ... aestatem seram ... autumno.
> (4.134-146)[12]

Finally, the inhabitants of Italy, Libya and Scythia are presented in similar terms (*genus acre virum*, 2.167; *non secus ac ... acer Romanus*, 3.346; *talis ... gens effrena virum*, 3.382). All of this should demonstrate the mechanical parallels between these passages, as well as Virgil's concern to depict the environments in comparative terms. What is the nature of these descriptions, and what is the result of the comparison?

It is fair to say that the traditional view of the *laudes Italiae*, apart from some recent exceptions,[13] has largely been a positive one; for instance:[14]

> The theme of *variety* and *spontaneity* – of happy cooperation between man and nature – is thus at last connected with the two other themes so dear to Virgil: the *Golden Age* and *Italy*. Italy, in short, is the actual realization of that mean or measure within the exuberant variety of nature which corresponds to the primal paradise before the Fall. As in other pictures of the Saturnian earth or age, we see the continual springtime, the exuberant

fertility, the absence of all that is horrible and monstrous (tigers, lions, poisons, snakes). And man is not here pitted against his environment in a fierce struggle for existence but forms, along with his works, the climactic essence of it:

173   Salve, magna parens frugum, Saturnia tellus,

174   magna virum.

It will be the suggestion here that the praises of Italy do not, in fact, contain an unmitigated approval. In two ways, by creating ambiguities about the environment with which he is dealing, and by departing from the tradition from which he drew, Virgil has subtly expressed severe reservations about his own national environment. This view can be tested against the ethnographical theory which forms the basis of Virgil's account, a theory whose importance for these lines has not yet been fully realized.

Examples of *laudes Italiae* abound. The quest for sources has been carried out by a number of critics,[15] with parallel descriptions found in Strabo (6.4.1),[16] Varro (*res rust.* 1.2.3-6; *ant. rer. hum.* 11),[17] Vitruvius (6.1.10-11), Dionysius of Halicarnassus (*Ant. Rom.* 1.36-37), Pliny (*N.H.* 3.39-42; 37.201-202) and Aelian (*V.H.* 9.16). Sophocles (*O.C.* 668-719) has even been suggested.[18] In fact, to this list we may perhaps add Cato (*ap.* Solinus 2.2).[19] So pervasive is the tradition, or it at least eventually became so, that Servius acknowledged it as a rhetorical *topos: iam incipit laus Italiae quam exsequitur secundum praecepta rhetorica: nam dicit eam et habere omnia bona et carere malis universis* (*ad Geo.* 2.136); for now judgement is suspended on the validity of Servius' view of Virgil's passage in this respect. It is noteworthy, however, that the versions of Pliny and Aelian, for instance, have lost the form of ethnographies, and definitely are to be seen as exaggerated pieces of rhetoric. The account of Strabo, on the other hand, is within the framework of an ethnographical study, and is therefore of a more scientific nature. In Virgil's passage also, although he omits or contracts certain elements which are unsuitable in a poetic setting (such as the elaborate treatment of *situs* which is found in Strabo's passage), the essential ethnographical format is intact.

With this tradition as a background, then, and noting in particular divergences from it, we should now examine Virgil's treatment of Italy. The first seven lines (136-142) set a contrast, treating foreign *thaumasia* – first positive, then negative. Italy surpasses all these exotic lands.[20] Here will be found none of the fabulous dangers of lands such as Colchis, where dragons' teeth yield a harvest of armed men.[21] Making this distinction, Virgil relates the real produce of Italy:

sed gravidae fruges et Bacchi Massicus umor

implevere; tenent oleae armentaque laeta.

(143-144)

Here, then, are the three basic agricultural categories, already referred to (pp. 35, 36, 38). The absence of apiculture is noticeable, again strengthening the distinction already made.[22] There is a further point to these lines; their terseness is striking. Such economy, particularly in this category, appears to be an integral part of the tradition (*ager frugum fertilis, bonus pecori, arbori infecundus*, Sall. *B.J.*17.5).[23] More importantly, in poetic versions these features consistently occur in the form of a couplet, as is the case here.[24] In Virgil's lines, the presence of these traditional elements, in great abundance (*gravidae ... implevere ... laeta*), suggests the completeness of the environment, and so far the description is consistent with other versions of *laudes Italiae*. What follows, however, is not:

> hinc bellator equus campo sese arduus infert,
> hinc albi, Clitumne, greges et maxima taurus
> victima, saepe tuo perfusi flumine sacro,
> Romanos ad templa deum duxere triumphos.
> (145-148)

The purpose of the horse is for warfare, that of the flocks and herds for military triumph. Such an emphasis has no place in the ethnographical tradition, and a very limited one even in the technical sections of the *Georgics*. The war-horse does appear in the third book, but only in passing (83-94). Again, the use of animals for triumphal sacrifice is hardly their most central function; indeed this function receives a mere half line in the 'didactic' part of the poem (*aut aris servare sacros*, 3.160). So, having given the purely conventional aspects of Italy's produce, Virgil departed from the tradition. We might expect elaboration dealing with the more agricultural functions of these animals (e.g. ploughing, wool, etc.); instead there is the suggestion only of warfare, sacrifice and military triumph.[25] These lines, moreover, are the first in a series in which Virgil has created a deliberate ambiguity between his hailing of Italy as *Saturnia tellus*, and the actual details of the land. It need scarcely be mentioned that warfare has little connection with the golden age (Hes. *W.D.* 189-193; Ovid *Met.* 1.98-100).

Treatment of Italy's climate follows:

> hic ver adsiduum atque alienis mensibus aestas:
> bis gravidae pecudes, bis pomis utilis arbos.
> (149-150)

The unusual fertility of the land results from its permanent springtime. What in fact is expected at this point is some reference to the *temperies* of Italy; in all other versions such detail is the focal point of this part of the description (Strabo 6.4.1; Varro *res rust.* 1.2.3-4; Dion. Hal. *Ant. Rom.* 1.37.5; Pliny *N.H.* 3.40; 37.201; Aelian *V.H.* 9.16; Vitr. 6.1.11). Servius clearly noted the discrepancy: *HIC VER ADSIDUUM: verna temperies; nam ver adsiduum esse non potest (ad Geo.* 2.149). The presence of this element is also expected as the cause of Italy's double productivity. As early as Hecataeus of Abdera, this connection had been made; so in his description of the Hyperboreans: φασιν ... ἔτι δ᾽ εὐκρασίᾳ διαφέρουσαν διττοὺς κατ᾽ ἔτος ἐκφέρειν καρπούς (Diod. 2.47.1 = *FGH* 264 fr. 7).

Why this departure from the tradition? It is noteworthy that while he does elsewhere use language suggesting the concept of *temperies* (*si non tanta quies iret frigusque caloremque/inter, et exciperet caeli indulgentia terras, Geo.* 2.344-345), Virgil never actually states the concept. Apart from the metrical restrictions in nominal forms of the term,[26] the explanation may lie in the very commonness of the idea; omission of the expression where it is virtually mandatory creates a particular emphasis.

In this instance, however, rather than omission, there is development of the concept from *temperies* to *ver adsiduum.* The genesis of this can be found in *Airs, Waters, Places,* where Asia Minor's climatic situation is closely approximated to that of spring: εἰκός τε τὴν χώρην ταύτην τοῦ ἦρος ἐγγύτατα εἶναι κατὰ τὴν φύσιν καὶ τὴν μετριότητα τῶν ὡρῶν, 12). Virgil has extended this observation, actually claiming for his environment the characteristic of eternal spring. Moreover, this claim, no less than the one for double productivity, is a patent falsehood.[27] Such features would constitute a denial of the idea, basic to the technical sections of the *Georgics,* that the mechanisms of the real agricultural world are dependent on the natural cycle of the seasons (1.252-258; 351-392; 2.315-345).[28] Nor is such a situation particularly a feature of the golden age; at least nowhere before the *Georgics* does it appear as such.[29] We should see the claim, then, as deliberate exaggeration, immediately recognizable to an audience familiar with the tradition of the *laudes Italiae.* The point of this exaggeration will emerge at a later stage.

At lines 151-154 Virgil has imposed on the Italian countryside a number of *thaumasia* from the golden age: there are no lions, tigers or snakes; poisonous plants are easily recognized and therefore harmless. Only two of these are in any sense true for the real Italy. This is, moreover, the only passage in the entire description which is consistent with a golden age setting. It is a combination of pure fiction and cliché (cf. *Ecl.* 4.21-25; *Geo.* 1.129; Hor. *Epode* 16.52), and is hardly sufficient to offset the contradictory elements which run through the remainder of the passage.[30]

Halfway through the description the emphasis changes. Virgil moves from a landscape largely characterized by natural features (lines 145-148, with their suggestions of warfare and triumphs, are the only exceptions) to one which is dominated and transformed by man. From this point, Virgil stresses the impact of civilized man on the natural setting of Italy, leaving behind the natural features which predominantly characterize the previous tradition of *laudes Italiae.*

First, the cities of Italy:

adde tot egregias urbes operumque laborem,
tot congesta manu praeruptis oppida saxis
fluminaque antiquos subter labentia muros.
(155-157)

Rivers are a natural enough element of ethnography, and they also regularly occur
in other versions of the praises of Italy. What is distinctive in these lines, however, is
the fact that the natural phenomena are presented in terms of the man-made
features which accompany them – in none of the other versions is this the case.
Virgil, then, has introduced into what is traditionally a natural environment a
feature which has no place in the natural world, namely the city. The phrase
congesta manu, moreover, emphasizes the idea of man's exertion, and possibly
even of his violence (cf. *Geo.* 3.32, 395; see Conington *ad loc.*).

And what of these lines in connection with the claim for Italy as a golden age
setting? Here Virgil himself is instructive; for, in the Fourth Eclogue, this very
feature – the walled city – was to be one of the remaining traces of a debased age in
his future golden period:[31]

pauca tamen suberunt priscae vestigia fraudis,
quae temptare Thetim ratibus, quae *cingere muris*
oppida, quae iubeant telluri infindere sulcos.
(*Ecl.* 4.31-33)

Ovid too (in terms which seem almost reminiscent of Virgil's) specifically excluded
this feature from his golden age:

nondum praecipites *cingebant oppida fossae*.
(*Met.* 1.97)

So, once again the Italian countryside is described in terms which appear to create a
deliberate contradiction with the claim that it is a Saturnian setting. Paratore seems
not to notice the tone of these lines when he likens them to those of Horace on the
stream of the Blessed Isles (*montibus altis/levis crepante lympha desilit pede,
Epode* 16.47-48).[32] This is the type of river we expect in a golden age landscape – not
one which is described in relation to a distinctly non-golden age phenomenon.

Next, in their correct place, come the seas, lakes and harbours of Italy:

an mare quod supra memorem, quodque adluit infra?
anne lacus tantos? te, Lari maxime, teque,
fluctibus et fremitu adsurgens Benace marino?
an memorem portus Lucrinoque addita claustra
atque indignatum magnis stridoribus aequor,
Iulia qua ponto longe sonat unda refuso
Tyrrhenusque fretis immittitur aestus Avernis?
(158-164)

Here is exactly the same movement as observed in lines 143-148. The first three verses treat the surrounding seas (the Adriatic and the Tuscan) and the country's lakes (Como and Garda). So far all is quite traditional; Strabo, Pliny and Aelian all treated these categories, emphasizing the natural beauty of these features. However, in the second half of this passage (*an memorem ...*), the same shift occurs as that detected in Virgil's treatment of the agricultural produce of Italy. Virgil proceeds to deal with the country's ports. As a general topic this is also traditional, but there is nothing resembling Virgil's specific stance in any of the other versions. For, after a very general opening (*an memorem portus*), he selects examples which are man-made and artificial (the Lucrine and the Avernus). Indeed the second of these is not even a harbour. Why such examples? Traditionally the lines have been seen as a glorification of the engineering feats of Julius Caesar and later Agrippa; but this may be a matter of pure extrapolation (from *Iulia ... unda*).[33] Surely the more plausible reading of the lines is that beneath any veneer of pride they convey a more negative impression. For elsewhere this very theme, the exclusion by artificial means of natural forces such as the sea, or man's imposition of himself upon such forces, stand as symptoms of the excesses which are seen to attend societies with an advanced level of civilization. At times these very examples – the Lucrine in particular – are used.[34] Virgil's language (*addita claustra ... indignatum magnis stridoribus aequor*) and his personification of the sea, emphasize the feeling of man's imposition, as does the resulting indignation of nature.

In fact, two details from the Servian commentaries combine to elucidate fully the force of Virgil's lines. First, Servius Auctus:

> 'indignatum' autem ideo dixit, quia quo tempore in Lucrinum lacum mare immissum est, deinde, terra effossa inter ipsum Lucrinum et Avernum, contigit, et duo lacus miscerentur, [et] tanta tempestas orta est, ut prodigii loco habita sit ac nuntiatum sit, simulacrum Averni sudasse.
> (Serv. Auct. *ad Geo.* 2.162)

Whether this happened or not is beside the point; what matters is that it is the natural result of such tampering. Man's interference with the forces of nature causes a violent reaction from these forces, together with a negative omen from the deity inhabiting the area.[35]

The second detail requires somewhat more elaborate explanation. At *Aeneid* 8.728 Virgil used the word *indignatus* as an epithet for the river Araxes (*pontem indignatus Araxes*), alluding, as had Herodotus (3.36) to the defeat of Cyrus the Great, which resulted from his crossing of that river.[36] Servius understood Virgil exactly:

> ARAXES: *hic* fluvius Armeniae quem pontibus nisus est Xerxes conscendere.
> (*ad Aen.* 8.728)

Now Xerxes had nothing to do with the Araxes. He is, however, the classic violator of the forces and boundaries of nature, and, as such, naturally came to Servius' mind as the object of the Araxes' *indignatio* – such an object being implicit in Virgil's phrasing. In the use of this same word in the *laudes Italiae* (in a parallel context) there are strong grounds for seeing criticism of the Roman achievement of creating these artificial lakes.[37]

Mention of the Lucrine and Avernus would also have conjured up, at least for an Augustan audience, the theme of *luxus;* for the two lakes were used as breeding-grounds for fish, an activity which was considered unnatural and paradigmatic of excessive wealth. Horace in particular (*Epode* 2.49-60; *Sat.* 2.4.32-34; *Ode* 2.15.1-4) saw this as the primary characteristic of the two lakes.[38] It is further significant that Horace later used these engineering accomplishments, again in a gnomic context, suggesting that whatever our wealth, whatever the splendour of our achievements, the strictures of mortality are unchanged:

> debemur morti nos nostraque; sive receptus
> terra Neptunus classis aquilonibus arcet,
> regis opus, sterilisve diu palus aptaque remis
> vicinas urbis alit et grave sentit aratrum,
> seu cursum mutavit iniquum frugibus amnis
> doctus iter melius, mortalia facta peribunt,
> nedum sermonum stet honos et gratia vivax.
> (*A.P.* 63-69)

In short, then, whereas he was able to take as examples of the harbours of Italy the large and natural instances (as, for example, was the procedure of Strabo: τὸ τοὺς ὄντας λιμένας μεγάλους εἶναι καὶ θαυμαστούς, 6.4.1), Virgil instead selected two which are artificial, and described them in language which suggests the imposition of civilized, technological man upon the forces of nature.

There follows a couplet on the mineral wealth of the land:

> haec eadem argenti rivos aerisque metalla
> ostendit venis atque auro plurima fluxit.
> (2.165-166)

The placement of these lines within the description of Italy is of interest. In ethnographical studies, a country's mineral resources are treated as a section of produce in general, and accordingly this feature is usually found with the agricultural category.[39] Virgil, however, has removed this feature from its natural position, and placed it in the second half of the passage together with those details which deal more with the effects of man on his environment. And here, from Virgil's point of view, is the appropriate place for these two lines; for the mention of precious metals, particularly of gold and silver, again suggests luxury,[40] and the presence of such metals implies a high degree of civilization and the potential for decline.[41] At the same time, the presence of bronze (*aerisque*) may carry a suggestion of warfare. Nor is this merely a poetic *topos*, confined to such seemingly moralistic writers as Horace. The same attitude is extremely common among ethnographical writers;[42] Tacitus in particular considered the pursuit of abundant mineral wealth to be a symptom of moral decay:

> argentum et aurum propitiine an irati dii negaverint dubito.
>
> *(Germ.* 5.3)
>
> nec quae natura quaeve ratio gignat, ut barbaris, quaesitum compertumve;
> diu quin etiam inter cetera eiectamenta maris iacebat, donec luxuria nostra dedit nomen.
>
> *(Germ.* 45.4)[43]

The first instance is perhaps ambivalent, but that in itself demonstrates that these elements are potentially negative. The second (Tacitus is talking of amber) is quite straightforward.

And what of these metals as part of a Saturnian land? Mining is hardly a feature of golden age societies;[44] indeed, Ovid was to assign it to the undesirable bronze age:

> sed itum est in viscera terrae,
> quasque reconditerat Stygiisque admoverat umbris,
> effodiuntur opes, irritamenta malorum.
> iamque nocens ferrum ferroque nocentius aurum
> prodierat.
>
> *(Met.* 1.138-142)

So, for the *laudes Italiae*, we again note detail which appears deliberately to contradict Virgil's final claim for the land, and to do so in a way suggesting the environment is less positive than is usually claimed.

At this point Virgil proceeds to the final *topos*, the description of the Italian *gentes*:

> haec genus acre virum, Marsos pubemque Sabellam
> adsuetumque malo Ligurem Volscosque verutos
> extulit, haec Decios Marios magnosque Camillos,
> Scipiadas duros bello et te, maxime Caesar,
> qui nunc extremis Asiae iam victor in oris
> imbellem avertis Romanis arcibus Indum.
>
> (167-172)

The inhabitants and their characteristics appear, as the tradition required, at the close of the description.

Virgil's is the only version of *laudes Italiae* to contain detail of this nature. Strabo deals primarily with purely Roman peoples, and other writers only briefly mention this category.[45] It is reasonable to assume that Virgil's details are dependent on no specific source, but are developed in accordance with his poetic purposes.

What is the significance of the lines? The climax of the description, they are marked by the same quality observed: deliberately negative departure from traditional material, and contradiction through detail of the final claim (*salve ... Saturnia tellus*). The first two lines are quite conventional, containing precisely the type of detail found in prose ethnographies.[46] The racial diversity of the original inhabitants, together with their distinguishing characteristics, is related. From this point, however, Virgil shifts ground – the pattern is exactly the same as at lines 145-148 (produce) and 161-164 (harbours) – and the final four lines are untraditional, dealing with specific individuals, rather than with peoples as a whole. This is the Virgilian transformation.

The emphasis in these final four lines is again on military activities. It has been recognized that Virgil, by stressing the warlike tendencies of the Romans while placing them in a temperate, prolific climate, has deliberately contradicted the Ionian view that a mild climate cannot produce inhabitants of a spirited or brave nature (οὐ γάρ τι τῆς αὐτῆς γῆς εἶναι καρπόν τε θαυμαστὸν φύειν καὶ ἄνδρας ἀγαθοὺς τὰ πολέμια, Herod. 9.122).[47] But what is the reason for this contradiction? If an accepted scientific theory is explicitly contradicted, we look for specific reasons. The implication seems to be that the Romans are military in nature *in spite of* the marvellous climate of Italy; the deliberate contradiction between the climatic conditions of the land and the nature of its inhabitants suggests that through their propensity for warfare the Romans have overcome the natural restrictions to which man in normal circumstances is subject.

Reynen and Borzsák,[48] in order to provide some mitigation of the seemingly excessive emphasis on militarism in these lines, turn to the passage on the praise of rural life at the end of the Second Georgic (458-540). In their view, the warrior of the *laudes Italiae* is to be combined with the rustic of those lines to create a composite of the Italian soldier-farmer. Clearly, before any evaluation of the former of these two passages can be made, the validity of this view must be tested; digression is called for.

The farmer at the end of the book in many ways resembles an inhabitant of the Saturnian land (this approximation seems unavoidable, cf. 459-460, 473-474, 500-502, 536-538); he has, however, little similarity to the inhabitant of the Italy of 2.136-176 – indeed, if, as we have claimed, that setting is deliberately anti-Saturnian in detail, we would expect no similarity; rather polarity, which is what we find. The farmer is not involved in wars or affairs of state (*flexit ... non res Romanae perituraque regna*, 498; *procul discordibus armis*, 458); surely the men of lines 169-172, if any, are representatives of *res Romanae* and of warfare. Like golden age man (*sine militis usu mollia securae peragebant otia gentes*, Ovid *Met.* 1.99-100), and unlike the figures of the *laudes Italiae*, this rustic has no part in wars at home or in foreign lands (503-504, 539-540). Unlike the inhabitant of Italy, he has no use for gold and wealth (498-499, 506-507). In contrast to the artificial falsehood of the climate in the *laudes Italiae*, this farmer is subject to the normal cycle of the seasons (*venit hiems*, 519). His lakes are natural (*vivique lacus* 469), in what appears to be a direct contrast to the Lucrine and Avernus.[49]

In short, rather than equating the two environments, we should see a direct and deliberate contrast between them. The claim that the idealized life of the rustic[50] is Saturnian (473-474, 536-538) is verified by the details of the description. In the *laudes Italiae*, the concluding lines,

> salve, magna parens frugum, Saturnia tellus,
> magna virum,

in that they hail the land as a golden age setting, are so much at variance with the actual details of the description that the reader is left uneasy; our view of Virgil's Italy cannot at this point be an entirely positive one.

To return to the treatment of *gentes*, then, the lines cannot be redeemed by having recourse to the end of the Second Georgic; they must stand as they are: a definite emphasis on Roman militarism. Some have claimed that each of the figures saved Rome from an external peril; but this cannot be the only, or even the primary, significance of a figure such as Marius.[51] The spectre of civil war and proscription was still close enough for mention of his name to produce an ambivalence about the 'heroes' of Rome's past. For the Roman of 29 BC, as for us, he is associated with brutality and despotism (the biographical tradition clearly reflects this, cf. Plut. *Marius* 2.1, 46.5).[52]

The phrase *Scipiadas duros bello* is also pointed; *duritia* is a concept prominent in ethnographical, as in biographical writings, denoting a certain primitive hardiness, assigned either to individuals or to races.[53] In this context it is much like *patientia*,[54] an even more prominent term, and one which Virgil implicitly applied to the Ligurians (*adsuetum malo*, 168). This same hardiness is assigned to the rustics at the end of the second book (*patiens operum exiguoque adsueta iuventus*, 472). Yet in these cases, and in ethnography in general, the quality is one of general endurance or hardiness. Virgil was later to use the word, in the context of a battle vaunt, when the Italian Numanus Remulus boasted to effeminate Trojan enemies:[55]

> at patiens operum parvoque adsueta iuventus
> aut rastris terram domat aut quatit oppida bello.
> (*Aen.* 9.607-608)

Even here the military sense is tempered by a more general one of endurance, or ability to survive. For the Scipios, however, the quality is purely military; Virgil has used a concept common in ethnographical treatments of *gentes*, but has done so in a sense which is atypical.

With this in mind, how do we approach the final two and a half lines of this category?

> et te, maxime Caesar,
> qui nunc extremis Asiae iam victor in oris
> imbellem avertis Romanis arcibus Indum.
>   (170-172)

Those critics who actually come to grips with these lines (and they are not numerous) see them (as they do *Geo.* 4.560-562) as implying that Octavian, by securing Rome's borders against the threat of foreign invasion, will establish another golden age in Italy – the familiar 'defensive imperialism'.[56] But such a view seems to be constructed without reference to Virgil's actual language; and here it is a question both of Latin and of the tradition behind the lines.

Specifically the problem rests in the phrase *imbellem avertis ... Indum.* Servius Auctus felt the dilemma:

> IMBELLEM AVERTIS: avertis et inbellem facis. an 'imbellem' victum iam, nec bellantem? ceterum quid grande, si inbellem avertis?
>   (*ad Geo.* 2.172)

What indeed, we concur. It seems a curious failing that at this point, the very climax of the *laudes Italiae*, a poet such as Virgil should fail so dismally to express himself clearly. And yet, if our claims for the description are valid, then these lines are no failure at all. Had Virgil wished to do so, he was quite capable of unambiguously stating "Octavian is now rendering the dangerous peoples of India powerless". But that was not his intention; rather, he has suggested (in necessarily ambiguous language) that the Roman military achievement, and the achievement of Octavian, its representative, is in some ways excessive and superfluous. This is surely the most natural sense: "Octavian is keeping the unwarlike Indian from the walls of Rome". The emphasis on distance, moreover (*extremis Asiae ... in oris*), is a further implication of the gratuitous nature of this activity.[57]

Yet on another level the words are totally free of any ambiguity. They can have only the negative sense which we favour. For it is impossible, if we realize the tradition of which Virgil's lines are consciously and unmistakably a part, that this more negative meaning was not intended. In a passage which is modelled on the form of ethnographical writing, and in which (as is always the case with ethnographical studies) the peoples of Italy are assigned various attributes of a permanent nature (*genus acre virum, adsuetumque malo Ligurem, Volscosque verutos,*[58] *Scipiadas duros bello*), *imbellem* can only be intended as a permanent, descriptive epithet. The peoples of the East here, as elsewhere in an ethnographical context, are specifically designated as being unwarlike:

> fertilis ager eoque abundans omnium copia rerum est regio, et *imbelles*, quod plerumque in uberi agro evenit, barbari sunt.
>   (Livy 29.25.12)[59]

The necessity of seeing this meaning in Virgil's lines exists only for a reader fully aware of the tradition of ethnography; Virgil appears ambiguous (as, presumably, he must), but in reality the meaning is quite clear.

It appears, then, that Virgil, in the *laudes Italiae*, developed and extended traditional material in such a way as to suggest that civilized Italy has crossed the limits imposed by nature. At the same time he has expressed severe reservations about empire and the Roman achievement. And finally, while ostensibly claiming that Italy in some way represents a renewal of the golden age, he has subtly proved the very opposite.[60]

All of this becomes clearer by citation of one critic who noted: "this noble tribute deserves at least a summary:

> But neither the forests of Media, wealthiest of lands, nor beautiful Ganges, nor Hermus running turbid with its gold, may vie with our Italy's praise; no, nor Bactra, nor India, nor all Panchaia, rich in incense-bearing sands. Teeming fruits have ever filled this land with the vine-god's juice from Mount Massic; it is the home of olives and of well-favored herds; from it come, Clitumnus, thy snow-white herds and bulls, noblest of victims, which oft bathed in thy sacred stream, have carried Romans in triumph to the temples of the gods. Here is unceasing springtide and summer in months not its own; twice yearly the cattle bear their young and twice do trees serve with their fruits. Add also Italy's many stately cities, the moil of our toiling, all those towns piled upon beetling crags, and streams that glide beneath time-honored walls. What need I tell of the seas that wash her shore, above and below? Or of her mighty lakes? This land of ours has shown currents of silver and copper and gold in her veins. She has been mother to vigorous races of men, the Marsian, the Sabine, the Ligurian inured to hardship, and the Volscian spearman. Hail land of Saturn, great mother of the fruits of earth, mighty mother of noble men".[61]

No warhorse, no golden age falsehoods, no indignant sea or land-locked Lucrine, no Marius and no gratuitously triumphant Octavian. This is the choice, it seems: either we ignore what seems to be less than laudatory, or we are required to conclude that Virgil, rather than simply praising the Italian landscape, has suggested that it exhibits serious deficiencies.

While, as noted at the outset of this chapter, it is not the task of this study to interpret the *Georgics* as a whole, it will be useful, before examining the other ethnographical descriptions of the poem, to indicate certain places in the technical material of the second book where the attitudes observed in the *laudes Italiae* appear to be reflected. This book is normally viewed as a "happy" one, the positive counterpoint to the clearly negative first and third books. There seem to be suggestions, however, throughout the book, that Virgil does not judge entirely positively man's attempts to regulate and tame the forces of nature; if this is the case, then the *laudes Italiae* may act as a mirror for the whole book.

The book begins, after a brief invocation, with the grafting of trees. Three passages are important:

> et saepe alterius ramos impune videmus
> vertere in alterius, mutatamque insita mala
> ferre pirum et prunis lapidosa rubescere corna.
>   (2.32-34)
>   ornusque incanuit albo
> flore piri glandemque sues fregere sub ulmis
>   (2.71-72)
>   nec longum tempus, et ingens
> exiit ad caelum ramis felicibus arbos,
> miratastque novas frondes et non sua poma.
>   (2.80-82)

Each of these passages appears at the close of a section on grafting, and to that extent can be seen as a climax of sorts. Virgil's emphasis on each is on the transformation which comes upon plants or trees as a result of man's grafting. These changes, moreover, are presented as agricultural *thaumasia*, and particularly in the last instance the language suggests that this is a strange and unnatural result (*miratastque*).[62] The tree, moreover, is personified, so as to be witness to the results of man's activities. This seems not very different from the personification of the sea in the *laudes Italiae*, and its indignation of the *claustra* imposed on it by man.

The conventional view of Virgil's attitude towards arboriculture and the contents of the Second Georgic is expressed by Otis:[63]

> "They [the trees] need some work but this is now taken quite joyfully for granted:
>
> 61   *scilicet* omnibus est labor impendendus et omnes
>   cogendae in sulcum ac multa mercede domandae".

Otis interprets from the tone created by *scilicet*, but to speak of joy in the context of these lines the reader must ignore the remainder of the couplet. Gerundives are not common in the corpus of Virgil.[64] Such tricolons of gerundives are positively rare; in fact, there are only four other instances, three in the second book of the *Georgics*, and all expressing the idea of force:[65]

> ipsa acie nondum falci temptanda, sed uncis
> carpendae manibus frondes interque legendae.
>   (2.365-366)
> terque quaterque solum scindendum glaebaque versis
> aeternum frangenda bidentibus, omne levandum
> fronde nemus.
>   (2.399-401)

sollicitanda tamen tellus pulvisque movendus
et iam maturis metuendus Iuppiter uvis.
                              (2.418-419)

In each the theme is the domination of nature by man, with the gerundives stressing
the idea. No happy co-operation here. The success of the second book is at times
qualified by Virgil's suggestion that after the Fall man must do violence to the
natural world, if he is to succeed in the world of *labor*. A coda: one critic has
remarked of *Geo.* 2.61-62: "the tempo is brisk and enthusiasm predominates".[66]
Now the first of these lines contains the phrase *labor impendendus*, the second is
entirely spondaic, with the exception of the fifth foot. As with the *laudes Italiae* so
here critics seem unwilling to consider the evidence provided by the poem itself.

The Third Georgic is generally acknowledged as being "dark". The climax of the
first half is a passage treating the destructive power of *amor*; attention lavished on
cattle and horses comes to nought, rendered futile by the onslaught of this *furor*
(209-283). Likewise, the plague at the end of the book (470-566) serves a similar
function; the forces of nature effectively negate the accomplishments of *labor*. In
the case of *amor* this destructive force is characterized by excessive heat (*in furias
ignemque ruunt*, 244; *continuoque avidis ubi subdita flamma medullis*, 271). The
same may be said of both the cause and effect of the plague, although here the
opposite element of cold is also involved (*ubi frigidus imber/altius ad vivum
persedit et horrida cano/bruma gelu, vel cum tonsis inlotus adhaesit/sudor, et
hirsuti secuerunt corpora vepres*, 441-444; *incertus ibidem/sudor et ille quidem
morituris frigidus*, 500-501; *ardentes papulae atque immundus olentia
sudor/membra sequebatur*, 564-565).

The motivating force for these failures is reflected in the ethnographical
descriptions of Libya and Scythia, each obviously representing an extreme in
temperature.[67] In fact, only the description of Scythia is a true ethnography, and it
is to that account that we should now turn. Its dependence on the form of
ethnographical writing has already been indicated (above, p. 37), and need not be
demonstrated again. Even in details, it is specifically from this tradition that Virgil
drew.[68] The description of intense cold (360-375), the account of waggons being
driven over frozen water (360-362), the concept of underground dwelling (376-383),
in short each of the elements of the description, is thoroughly traditional. Nor
should we look for a specific locale behind the account; Virgil has presented what is
virtually a paradigm for the wintry north.[69]

Most of the details, then, need little elaboration. The emphasis throughout is on
the constant, restrictive cold of the Scythian landscape.[70] It is this cold which
regulates man's activities, and sets the land in clear contrast to the eternal spring of
Italy in the second book. Here winter is continuous (*semper hiems, semper
spirantes frigora Cauri*, 355), as spring was in the *laudes Italiae* (*hic ver adsiduum*,
2. 149).[71] Conventional agricultural pursuits are here restricted (*illic clausa tenent*

stabulis armenta, 352) or impossible (*neque ullae/aut herbae campo apparent aut arbore frondes*, 352-353), while in Italy their development was complete, as it is in all civilized lands (*sed gravidae fruges et Bacchi Massicus umor/implevere; tenent oleae armentaque laeta*, 2.143-144). Again the parallels in diction (here the same tripartite division) can hardly be accidental.[72]

It will be our suggestion that this contrast does not work entirely to the credit of Italy, nor to the total detriment of the Scythian landscape. Rather, both are to some extent flawed, although for opposite reasons. The Scythians, in spite of the extent to which they are impeded by their harsh climate, do manage to acquire the necessities of existence without undue difficulty; indeed, the very snow which causes the death of the animals (368-370) works to man's advantage, in that it allows him to hunt with relative ease (371-375).

But it is specifically in the closing lines of the account that the point is made; here Virgil presented a vivid picture of the Scythians, at ease in the caverns which serve as their shelters:

> ipsi in defossis specubus secura sub alta
> otia agunt terra, congestaque robora totasque
> advolvere focis ulmos ignique dedere.
> hic noctem ludo ducunt, et pocula laeti
> fermento atque acidis imitantur vitea sorbis.
> talis Hyperboreo Septem subiecta trioni
> gens effrena virum Riphaeo tunditur Euro
> et pecudum fulvis velatur corpora saetis.
>
> (3.376-383)

As with hunting, so with their living conditions, the Scythians are, to some extent, able to overcome the rigours of their environment and to use its features to their advantage. Some critics have in fact recognized that the picture is not as bleak as the conditions would seem to call for.[73] Man has here adapted himself to his natural surroundings, and thereby achieved a harmony of sorts with nature. This too appears in deliberate contrast to the moulding of nature as noted in the *laudes Italiae*. The life of the Scythian is one in which *otium* is predominant (*secura sub alta/otia agunt terra*, 371-372); the inhabitants of Italy, with their concern for military enterprises, are implicitly excluded from such a world.

More importantly, *otium* is one of the attributes of the idealized rustic of the second book (468), a figure who, as we have claimed, is depicted in direct contrast to the Italian of the *laudes Italiae*. This line should be pursued somewhat further, for Virgil seems to have consciously equated the Scythian and the rustic:

> at *secura quies* et nescia fallere vita,
> dives opum variarum, at latis *otia* fundis,
> *speluncae* vivique lacus.
>
> (2.467-469)[74]

ipsi in defossis *specubus secura* sub alta
otia agunt terra.

(3.376-377)

The farmer's peaceful life is attained with the help of a beneficent environment; the Scythian, in spite of his environment, achieves a very similar peace. Accepting the scene at the end of the Second Georgic as the setting which comes closest of any to the golden age (cf. 473-474, 536-538), we may observe that in some respects the society of the Scythians has similar affinities. In the next detail of the Scythian description, the people are seated around a fire, occupied in play and the drinking of beer:[75]

congestaque robora totasque
advolvere focis ulmos ignique dedere.
hic noctem ludo ducunt et pocula laeti
fermento atque acidis imitantur vitea sorbis.

(3.377-380)

They must make do with beer, but it serves them as well as wine. And what of the rustic Italian's picnic?

ipse dies agitat festos fususque per herbam,
ignis ubi in medio et socii cratera coronant,
te libans, Lenaee, vocat pecorisque magistris
velocis iaculi certamina ponit in ulmo,
corporaque agresti nudant praedura palaestra.

(2.527-531)

In both scenes, then, we have a camp-fire, play and drinking. In short, it is the Scythian, not the Roman of the *laudes Italiae*, who has affinities to the idealized farmer of *Georgics* 2.

Finally in this connection, it is worth noting the phrase: (*gens*) *Hyperboreo Septem subiecta trioni* (381). Metaphorically, the epithet *Hyperboreo* of course denotes the far north. But Virgil may intend, through its literal meaning, a suggestion of the Hyperboreans, that mythical race which appears in Herodotus (4.32-36), and whose Utopian society was treated by Hecataeus of Abdera.[76] This too, then, may constitute a redeeming detail.

Such is the life of the Scythians (*talis ... gens effrena virum*). This expression suggests the primitive harshness which is a quality of uncivilized societies (Sall. *B.J.* 17.6; Virg. *Aen.* 8.315). It is, moreover, a quality which was viewed positively, and in contrast to the softness which exists in more advanced cultures. In addition there is, in these words, a connection with the quality of *patientia*, which, as we saw, was a feature shared both by the contented rustic (*Geo.* 2.472) and the early Latins (*Aen.* 9.607). Their ability to survive in such an extreme climate qualifies the Scythians to be included in this group. Although the term is also reminiscent of the Latins in the *laudes Italiae* (*genus acre virum*, 2.167), this group is to be distinguished in that Virgil developed and emphasized the military nature of their endurance to the exclusion of any other, more general quality.

The contrast between the *laudes Italiae* and the description of Scythia presents itself on the level of syntax, diction and form. In the former Virgil depicted an artificially benevolent environment, then proceeded, by extending and colouring the detail of that environment, to express doubts about its inhabitants and the extent to which they had pursued their technological goals. The result was a moulding and transforming of their natural setting. In the account of Scythia he presented a landscape in which the exaggerated harshness of nature had compelled man to subject himself to her. In a movement which is parallel to but the reverse of that detected in the *laudes Italiae*, Virgil has demonstrated the Scythian's acceptance of nature's domination, and how, without altering his natural environment or forcing it to conform to his wishes, he has learnt to live with reasonable ease within the limits it imposes. Neither setting is ultimately successful, but the terms of failure are reversed from one account to the other.

Horace, I believe, detected and commented upon Virgil's view:

> Intactis opulentior
> thesauris Arabum et divitis Indiae
>   caementis licet occupes
> Tyrrhenum omne tuis et mare Apulicum,
>   si figit adamantos   5
> summis verticibus dira Necessitas
>   clavos, non animum metu,
> non mortis laqueis expedies caput.
>   campestres melius Scythae,
> quorum plaustra vagas rite trahunt domos,   10
>   vivunt et rigidi Getae,
> immetata quibus iugera liberas
>   fruges et Cererem ferunt,
> nec cultura placet longior annua,
>   defunctumque laboribus   15
> aequali recreat sorte vicarius.
>   illic matre carentibus
> privignis mulier temperat innocens,
>   nec dotata regit virum
> coniunx nec nitido fidit adultero.   20
>   dos est magna parentium
> virtus et metuens alterius viri
>   certo foedere castitas;
> et peccare nefas aut pretium est mori.
>   (*Odes* 3.24.1-24)

Here the uncivilized Scythian is seen in favourable opposition to the poet's own society. The latter's concern with amassing wealth and building out into the sea are particularly condemned.[77] Indeed, in lines 3-4 (*caementis licet occupes/ Tyrrhenum omne tuis et mare Apulicum*), although the activity implied is slightly different, it is difficult not to see *Geo.* 2.161-164 – the barriers imposed on the Lucrine, and the Tuscan Sea released into the Avernus. Both are acts against the natural world.

In keeping with his more moralistic persona, Horace is even more emphatic than Virgil in his insistence on the ethical superiority of the Scythians: *campestres melius Scythae*. Horace was clearly familiar not only with the Virgilian context, but also independently with the ethnographical tradition from which Virgil drew in his Scythian account. For he portrayed these people as nomadic (*quorum plaustra vagas rite trahunt domos*, 10), perhaps the most prevalent feature in the tradition,[78] but one not mentioned by Virgil (although he does assign them *plaustra*, 2.362). Also traditional is the detail that they change their pasture each year, and work the fields in common.[79]

Through these ethnographical details, Horace subtly makes a transition which again is relevant to our discussion of Virgil; the attributes given to the Scythians are not unlike those which Horace elsewhere assigns to the virtuous inhabitants of early Italy. Here, as in *Epode* 2.39-48 and in the Roman Odes (particularly 3.2 and 3.6), the ideal Scythian *virtus* is cast in the same terms as that of the morally upright Sabine. The emphasis is on maternal duty, marital fidelity and filial piety.[80] Elsewhere, the equation seems even more deliberate (*rigidis ... Sabinis, Epist.* 2.1.25; cf. *rigidi Getae, Odes* 3.24.11).[81] For the Scythians this adjective is particularly appropriate, and in it there may be a slightly ironical reference to Virgil's passage (*vestesque rigescunt/indutae, Geo.* 3.363-364).

Moral superiority, then, of a less civilized race. This is also implied in the similarities which Horace seems to suggest between the Scythian and the inhabitants of the golden age. Like the latter in the First Georgic (*ne signare quidem aut partiri limite campum fas erat*, 1.126-127) Horace's Scythians have fields without boundaries (*immetata*, 12), and like the produce in Virgil's passage (*liberius nullo poscente*, 129) that of Horace's Scythia is also described as *liber* (*iugera liberas/fruges et Cererem ferunt*, 12-13).[82]

In some ways Horace appears as a commentator on the attitude of Virgil in these two formal ethnographical descriptions. The two passages[83] stand in a chiastic relationship:

laudes Italiae	– apparently positive environment with negative detail refuting claims for approximation to golden age.
Scythia	– apparently negative environment with redeeming detail suggesting approximation to golden age.

Ultimately both environments are condemned, although the reasons for the condemnation are opposite. By the end of the Third Georgic, Virgil has presented two structurally parallel landscapes, whose basis is in the tradition of ethnographical writings, and which represent, in a sense, opposite alternatives. The ideal has become negative, the untenable tolerable. Finally, however, both settings are flawed.

The passage on the old man of Tarentum, which has formal parallels to the *laudes Italiae* and the Scythian excursus, and which, like them, has a basis in ethnographical writing (above, p. 37), offers a viable alternative to these settings, and one whose implications are crucial for an understanding of the poem.

With some exceptions, the account has received little attention.[84] The reasons are not difficult to find: the fact that it is presented as an "excursus" from the important treatment of the bee society, and that the digressional stance is stressed by elaborate framing *praeteritiones* (4.116-124, 147-148) help to create the impression that this scene is as gratuitous from the poetic standpoint as it appears misplaced or insignificant from the technical aspect. The overall division of the four books excludes the category of gardens, although, of course, they had been treated in previous technical treatises.[85]

Virgil first locates his setting:

> namque sub Oebaliae memini me turribus arcis,
> qua niger umectat flaventia culta Galaesus,
> Corycium vidisse senem
>
> (4.125-127)

Presentation of the landscape through mention of a river recalls the opening of the *laudes Italiae* (*auro turbidus Hermus ... totaque turiferis Panchaia pinguis harenis*, 2.137-139),[86] and, even more strongly, the beginning of the Scythian description:

> at non qua Scythiae gentes Maeotiaque unda,
> turbidus et torquens flaventis Hister harenas
>
> (3.334-350)

The *situs* is given, then, and in a manner which from the very outset binds the passage to the other ethnographical *logoi* of the poem.

At this point light can perhaps be shed on a long-puzzled question: Who is this Corycian? From Servius on the question has been asked, with various answers. He suggested one of the Cilician pirates settled by Pompey, rejecting in the process what seems to have been a variant explanation (*qui more Corycio hortos excoluit, ad Geo*. 4.127). Servius Auctus adds that Cilicians were good gardeners – clearly an extrapolation. Other candidates are Meliboeus of the Third Eclogue, Valerius Cato and a neo-Pythagorean from Tarentum.[87] None of these suggestions is satisfactory, in that they all require information from outside the context of Virgil's poem; or, to put it otherwise, they are all symptoms of a biographical approach to the poem. If the word has any sense, it must have it within the context of Virgil's description. Now if, as I think has been shown, Virgil intended this passage to be viewed as parallel to the other ethnographical sequences of the *Georgics*, and if at least in form it *is* an ethnography, then *Corycium ... senem* makes ideal sense: the old man was originally from Cilicia; – that, and that alone, is the point of the adjective. For, as a glance at Sallust's Libyan ethnography will show (*B.J.* 18-19), the origins of a country's inhabitants are a vital part of ethnographical study.[88] So Tacitus' *Germania* was in fact entitled *de origine et situ Germanorum.*[89] By making his subject a Corycian, then, Virgil has again indicated the tradition from which he drew, at the same time enforcing the connection to his other ethnographical passages.[90]

The description of the old man's plot begins with a dismissal of conventional agricultural pursuits, once more in terms of the familiar tricolon:

> cui pauca relicti
> iugera ruris erant nec fertilis illa iuvencis
> nec pecori opportuna seges nec commoda Baccho.
> hic rarum tamen ...
>
> (4.127-130)[91]

In the *laudes Italiae* these categories were present in abundance, and in contrast (syntactically parallel to, and the reverse of, the present lines) to the exotic and fabulous *thaumasia* of foreign lands (*haec loca non ... sed gravidae fruges, etc.* 2.140-144). The uses to which they were put, however, indicated an excessively technological and militaristic society (lines 145-148; above, pp. 38-51). In the description of Scythia, as for the Tarentine, such pursuits were ruled out by the climatic harshness (3.352-353); in their place was snow, ice and impeding cold (*sed iacet ...* 354-355) – parallel syntax again. There only the relatively primitive practice of hunting could exist.

Synthesis is called for. In the first three books of the *Georgics* Virgil expressed reservations about the success of these three conventional agricultural pursuits of civilized man. In Books 1 and 3 these arts were swept away at the hands of natural forces (storms, civil war, *amor* and the plague). In Book 2, as we suggested, the negation is more subtle. There, to attain any degree of success man was forced to impose himself upon, and distort, the elements of nature. Virgil's attitude towards this "success" has already been suggested. The agricultural sections of Virgil's ethnographical passages reflect this larger outlook.

If Virgil's attitude to the Corycian's landscape is a positive one, then (considering the dictional parallels), his specific removal of these three elements from the old man's plot appears to stand as his acknowledgement of failure of civilized agricultural activity, and ultimately as his criticism of societies involved in such activities. What does the old man produce?

> hic rarum tamen in dumis olus albaque circum
> lilia verbenasque premens vescumque papaver

regum aequabat opes animis, seraque revertens
nocte domum dapibus mensas onerabat inemptis.
(4.130-133)

A few vegetables, a herb-garden for seasoning, flowers for honey, and the
occasional fruit-tree (142-143).[92] With this little he is self-sufficient; indeed, more
than self-sufficient (*regum aequabat opes animis*). While elsewhere in the poem
large-scale agricultural endeavour appears subject to failure, in a private and
individual sphere success is possible.

This is a world distinct from any in Virgil's poetry; once, earlier in the *Georgics*,
he had briefly hinted that this was to come:

laudato[93] ingentia rura,
exiguum colito.
(2.412-413)[94]

This advice is realized in the setting of the old man of Tarentum. The emphasis here
on individual self-sufficiency is atypical of Virgilian thought; it is more a feature of
Horace's poetry. Where Virgil tended to dwell on darker and more cosmic orders,
Horace accepted the world's shortcomings and replaced them with his own private
world. It is small wonder, then, that, as we showed in the last chapter, Horace
recalled these very lines of Virgil in a poem displaying the superiority of that private
world (*Epistle* 1.16). That he did so in the form of an ethnographical description
allied his world to that of *Geo.* 4.125-148; at the same time it represents his
acknowledgement of the whole construct we have traced through the *Georgics*.[95]

The climate of the old man's setting is also distinct from, and distinguished from,
those of the previous ethnographical passages:

primus *vere* rosam atque *autumno* carpere poma,
et cum tristis *hiems* etiamnum frigore saxa
rumperet et glacie cursus frenaret aquarum,
ille comam mollis iam tondebat hyacinthi
aestatem increpitans seram Zephyrosque morantis.
(4.134-138)

Here is the real world, with the various seasons acting as they do in the technical
sections of the poem, and acting as Virgil knew them to act, even in climatically
benign Italy. This landscape is thus distinguished equally from the destructive
continual winter of Scythia and from the artificial (and deliberately false) eternal
spring of the *laudes Italiae*. The Corycian's success is in real terms, and to that
extent it is the only such success in the poem.[96] Through his individual efforts, and
in seclusion from the public world of the *Georgics*, he has reached a state of
harmony with the reality of the natural world.

If we accept the importance of this episode, we can begin to see the central position held by Tarentum, not only for Virgil, but for subsequent Augustan poetry. It stands virtually as a paradigm for the exclusive world of the poet. Horace, in *Odes* 2.6, chose it as the ideal place for his old age (*meae sedes ... senectae*, 5),[97] surely thereby associating not only his setting with that of Virgil, but also himself with Virgil's character (*Corycium ... senem*). Specific reference is strengthened by Horace's use of the river by which Virgil referred to the old man's landscape, the Galaesus (*dulce ... Galaesi/flumen, Odes* 2.6.20-21).

The next appearance of this word in Latin poetry (and thereafter it did not occur until Statius and Martial) is also relevant:

> tu canis umbrosi subter pineta Galaesi
> Thyrsin et attritis Daphnin harundinibus.
> (Prop. 2.34.67-68)

Propertius is cataloguing Virgil's poetic production; these lines refer to the *Eclogues* specifically. Now neither the Galaesus nor Tarentum appears in the *Eclogues*.[98] The reference seems to be unmistakably to the passage from the Fourth Georgic (cf. *umbras*, 4.146).[99] The most likely explanation for such a transference on the part of Propertius is that to him also the lines of Virgil described a setting very different in tone and import from the rest of the *Georgics*. While the scene is not precisely pastoral, it does, for instance, as has been noted,[100] have certain affinities to the First Eclogue. But essentially it is the positive nature and tranquility of the Tarentine landscape which leads Propertius to place the Virgil of the *Eclogues* in it.

At the same time Virgil's attitude towards Tarentum is thoroughly consonant with the poetic programme of Callimachean/Augustan verse. We can detect in the triumph of the old man's small plot over the large world of agriculture the metaphorical continuance of those Callimachean principles to which Virgil stated his allegiance in the Sixth Eclogue. Here too *Geo.* 2.412-413 is relevant: *laudato ingentia rura, exiguum colito*. As much as anything else, this is the language of a poetic creed.[101]

Again Horace is the best commentator:

> parvum parva decent: mihi iam non regia Roma,
> sed vacuum Tibur placet aut imbelle Tarentum.
> (*Epist.* 1.7.44-45)
> mihi parva rura et
> spiritum Graiae tenuem Camenae
> Parca non mendax dedit et malignum
> spernere vulgus.
> (*Odes* 2.16.37-40)

Here is the whole picture. In the first passage *regia Roma* (the Rome of the *laudes Italiae*?) is unfavourably contrasted to *imbelle Tarentum* (the Tarentum of the

Fourth Georgic?), with *vacuum Tibur* (Horace's own poetic landscape?) favourably implicated. The preference is both ethical and poetical, as the opening words show: *parvum parva decent* – this can scarcely be other than a statement of poetic preference.[102] If there is doubt it is removed by the second passage. There the rural metaphor (*parva rura*) is openly combined with a poetic one (*spiritum Graiae tenuem Camenae*), with both presented in the setting of a Callimachean programme.[103]

Burck sees in the description of the old man's landscape a reflection of the world of the bees, in which, of course, it is set.[104] It is now time to turn to their society.

NOTES

1. B. Otis, Appendix 6, 407.

2. "Die Komposition von Vergils *Georgika*", *Hermes* 64 (1929) 279-321.

3. *Virgils Georgica*, Bibl. der Alten Welt, Forschung und Deutung (Zurich 1963) 15 (= Entretiens sur l'Antiquité Classique II [Vandoeuvres-Genève 1953] 149); for similar sentiments see Richter 8-9.

4. Bee-keeping was obviously felt by Varro also to be something of an appendage to the more serious agricultural pursuits: *nos mel neclegemus* (*res rust.* 3.16) he notes in his introduction to the subject. Cf. too Richter on *Geo.* 2.143ff., 223.

5. The poetic function of Virgil's bees in the *Georgics* will be the subject of the next chapter.

6. Incidentally, if any argument remains about the authenticity of this closing *sphragis*, this occurrence of a typical agricultural tricolon should settle the matter; or else the interpolator too was familiar with the requirements of the ethnographical tradition.

7. Cf. A. S. F. Gow and A. F. Scholfield, edd. *Nicander* (Cambridge 1953) 209; they rightly attach little importance to a statement of Quintilian (*Nicandrum frustra secuti Macer atque Vergilius? Inst.* 10.1.56), which is probably intended only in the most general sense. They are also doubtless correct in doubting Kroll's claim ("Nikandros", *RE* 17.255) that the extant fragments are not representative of the whole work in that they were compiled mainly by Athenaeus, whose concerns were of a specialized nature. In general, for the importance of Nicander, see Klingner (above, n. 3, "Einleitung"), who views the Hellenistic poet as one (although an important one) of a number of writers influential on Virgil.

8. "Une Source de Virgile dans les Georgiques", *REL* 16 (1938) 297-317; his own views are preceded by a useful summary of the possible influences.

9. We cannot, of course, claim with full assurance that Virgil's arrangement does not reflect that of one of the numerous previous writers of agronomical treatises (for whom see Varro, *res rust.* 1.1.8-11), although it is unlikely, I think, that any of these unnotables could have so influenced Virgil.

10. So Dahlmann, *passim*. His views, and subsequent critical reaction to them, will be examined in the next chapter.

11. The comparative brevity of the account of the Libyan herdsmen (which is something of a puzzle) and its lack of formal ethnographical development really set it outside our study (although see below, n. 83). R. Martin ("Virgile et la Scythie", *REL* 44 [1966] 286-304) believes this discrepancy is resolved by recognizing that the Scythian passage was expanded after information about the area was brought back to Rome following an expedition to Moesia in 29 B.C. This is not, however, particularly convincing, for the detail in Virgil's description is quite traditional. As will become evident, moreover, the entire account is integral to the *Georgics*, and must therefore have been a part of the poem well before 29.

12. This final instance is very different from the other two; the nature of this difference will emerge in the course of this chapter.

13. The first study to suggest that the *laudes Italiae* may not convey an altogether positive view of the land was that of M. C. J. Putnam, "Italian Virgil and the Idea of Rome", in *Janus, Essays in Ancient and Modern Studies* (Ann Arbor 1975) 171-199; also, since the original writing of the present work, C. Perkell, *Pessimism in the Georgics of Virgil* (diss. Harvard 1977); M. C. J. Putnam, *The Georgics: Virgil's Poem of the Earth* (Princeton 1979). Neither of these deals with the episode in terms of the tradition which is our subject. I hope, by examining it against an identifiable tradition, to remove some of the subjectivity which might otherwise intrude.

14. Otis 164; for a similar view, see L. P. Wilkinson, *The Georgics of Virgil* (Cambridge 1969) 87. Full bibliography is hardly necessary here, so prevalent is the opinion.

15. Notably J. Geffcken, "Saturnia Tellus", *Hermes* 27 (1892) 381-388; he does not include, perhaps in that he is more concerned with possible sources only, Vitruvius (here see Norden, *Die germanische Urgeschichte* 111, n. 1), or Cato (see below, n. 19).

16. Strabo's account should be given precedence over the others, if we accept Geffcken's argument (382-383) that it was drawn from Polybius and Posidonius; if this is the case then it is interesting that the laudatory tone of these descriptions seems to have been a part of the tradition from an early stage: ὑφ' ὧν νῦν εἰς τοσοῦτον ὕψος ἐξήρθησαν Ῥωμαῖοι (Strabo 6.4.1).

17. Recognized by P. Mirsch, "De M. Ter. Varronis antiquitatum rerum humanarum libris XXV", *Leipz. Stud.* 5 (1882) 34, 111-114; also Geffcken 383, and Norden, *Die germanische Urgeschichte* 111, n. 1 (where Varro's passage is seen as the link between Posidonius and Vitruvius). Little can be said of this as a comprehensive model.

18. By A. H. Krappe, "A Source of Vergil, *Georg.* II.136-176", *CQ* 20 (1926) 42-44. Unaware of the details of the ethnographical tradition, he sees Sophocles as a possible source for Virgil in his treatment of olives, cattle and rivers (which do not appear in Varro's treatment).

19. Solinus' claim is somewhat remarkable, especially since, after naming Cato as the author of a *laudes Italiae*, he gives all the ethnographical categories (*caeli temperies*, etc.); although the actual language is doubtless that of Solinus, it is contrary to all indications that knowledge of this tradition was disseminated in Rome before the time of Posidonius, or certainly of Polybius (it may, however, have been a late work of Cato's).

20. R. Fischer (*Das ausseritalische geographische Bild in Vergils Georgica, in den Oden des Horaz und in den Elegien des Properz* [diss. Zurich 1968] 13-15) points out that these foreign lands correspond, in

reverse order, to those mentioned in the preceding lines (109-135) dealing with the variety of different countries. This being so, it is noteworthy that Virgil has deliberately brought about a link between technical material and "excursus".

21. Paratore (*Introduzione alle Georgiche* [Palermo 1938] 55-56) sees a parallel here, as elsewhere (his other theories will be dealt with as they arise), with Horace, *Epodes* 16.57-58. The emphasis there, however, is more on the decline associated with navigation (the Argo), and on the destructive immorality of Medea (*impudica Colchis*). Virgil is merely concerned with the *thaumasia* associated with Jason's ordeal, not with making any moral comparisons.

22. See Richter, *ad loc.*, for bare notice of this omission.

23. Cf. above, Introduction, p. 3; other instances: Caesar, *B.G.* 12.3; 14.2; Tacitus, *Agr.* 12.5; *Germ.* 5.1. For a rhetorical expansion of this practice, see Dion. Hal. *Ant. Rom.* 1.37.

24. Horace, *Epist.* 1.16.2-3 (see above, p. 12); Virg. *Geo.* 2.222-223; 3.352-353; 4.128-129; 4.559-560; Lucan 9.433-434 (this occurrence will be relevant in our discussion in Chapter 5). The poetic instances are restricted to these poets, the three who drew from the ethnographical tradition.

25. The terms "militarism" and "imperialism" will be used without apology in what follows. Although definition of the Roman attitude towards these phenomena is difficult (and, doubtless, no single attitude existed, as none does for us), it seems totally perverse to deny that *some* attitude towards such issues could be formulated by a troubled poet living in a sophisticated society. E. Badian puts it best, attributing the rejection of imperialistic concerns to two motivations, the *utile* or the *honestum*: "The individual may realise that the pursuit of his ambition may be bad for his health or happiness; or he may come to question the principle of competition and the pursuit of power and distinction as a motive force. Similarly the community. We are not going to be concerned with the *merits* of this ... Our point is only that both these motives, in their different ways, are signs of sophistication, overcoming the deep-seated urge for domination and power" (*Roman Imperialism in the Late Republic*, 2nd ed. [Oxford 1968, Ithaca 1971] 1). For the view that Virgil felt positively towards imperialism, together with a useful bibliography on the subject outside poetry, see H. Reynen, "Ewiger Frühling und goldene Zeit, Zum Mythos des goldenen Zeitalters bei Ovid und Vergil", *Gymnasium* 72 (1965) 427-428.

26. Cf. above, Chapter 1, p. 11.

27. *Biferitas* is usually claimed for single, aberrant plants, trees or groves, and seems to be a result of cult association (e.g., Theophr. *hist. plant.* 1.9.5; Varro, *res rust.* 1.7.6). I know of no instance before Virgil where this is claimed as a regular feature of a purportedly real environment. Richter points to Varro's pigs as a parallel (*res rust.* 2.3.4, 2.4.14), but Virgil's *pecudes* is clearly inclusive of larger animals (cf. *Geo.* 2.340, 3.243, 3.368; *Aen.* 1.743) for which such prolificness is obviously ruled out. Dionysius of Halicarnassus, incidentally, went one better than Virgil: ... τὰ καλούμενα Καμπανῶν πεδία, ἐν οἷς ἐγὼ καὶ τρικάρπους ἐθεασάμην ἀρούρας (*Ant. Rom.* 1.37.2).

28. In Virgil's *atque alienis mensibus aestas* Conington (*ad loc.*) suggests a reminiscence of Lucretius (*quod si de nihilo fierent, subito exorerentur/incerto spatio atque alienis partibus anni*, 1.180-181). If this reminiscence is "meaningful" then the parallel would support the view that Virgil intended his claim to be recognized as a falsehood.

29. So Reynen (above, n. 25) 419-426. He demonstrates that the concept, linked specifically with the golden age, does not appear before Ovid (*Met.* 1.107-108), who doubtless adopted it from the *laudes*

Italiae. For an unquestioning belief that *ver adsiduum* is a traditional feature of the golden age, see N. Deratini, "Virgile et l'âge d'or", *RPh* 5 (1931) 129; Paratore (above, n. 21) 53-54; Richter, *ad loc.* The relationship between Virgil's passage and the tradition of the golden age will be treated as the issue arises.

30. In any case, and this is important for the entire poem, the golden age is, in the *Georgics*, a thing of the past; that is unequivocally stated by Virgil early in the poem (1.121-149). Success in such terms is no success at all in terms of the world this poem examines. As D. O. Ross has put it (*Backgrounds to Augustan Poetry* [Cambridge 1975] 105, n. 4): "the golden Saturnian age cannot be reconciled either with the *labor* of Virgil's real country or with the real world, *res Romanae peritaraque regna*".

31. Lucretius also excluded cities from his early period (5.1108), although for him, of course, this was hardly a positive feature.

32. Paratore (above, n. 21) 54; his broader equating of the two passages will not stand scrutiny: Virgil's produce is qualitatively distinct from that of the Sixteenth Epode (which is characterized by a spontaneity consistent with a Utopian or Saturnian setting). Only in the absence of snakes (mere commonplace) is there any real similarity between the two environments. The common dependence on the ethnographical tradition gives the impression of a more significant parallel, but it is through deviation of detail within this form that in fact a distinction is created between the two settings.

33. Servius (*ad Geo.* 2.161) is the sole source for this attribution.

34. Generally: Horace, *Odes* 3.1.33-34, 3.24.3; Seneca the Elder, *Contr.* 5.5; Seneca the Younger, *Tranq.* 3.7; with specific reference to the Lucrine and the Bay of Naples: Horace, *Odes* 2.15.1-4, 2.18.20-22. See now R. G. M. Nisbet and M. Hubbard (*A Commentary on Horace: Odes Book II* [Oxford 1978]) in their introduction to both poems.

35. For the sweating of statues as an unpropitious omen, see F. B. Krauss, *An Interpretation of the Omens, Portents and Prodigies recorded by Livy, Tacitus and Suetonius* (diss. Univ. of Pennsylvania 1930) 94, 108, 176ff.

36. On the literary function in Herodotus, see H. Immerwahr, *Form and Thought in Herodotus*, APhA Monographs 23 (1966) 75.

37. There is a curious comment by Servius Auctus on *Aen.* 8.728: *cui [flumini] Alexander Magnus pontem fecit, quem fluminis incrementa ruperunt. postea Augustus firmiore ponte eum ligavit, unde ad Augusti gloriam dixit 'pontem indignatus Araxes'.* And on Agrippa's engineering feats in the *laudes Italiae: verum huius (operis) gloria Augusto cessit* (*ad Geo.* 2.162). The first of these is patent nonsense; Augustus was never even near the Araxes (nor was Alexander for that matter). What, then, is the point? The Servian commentaries at both instances of *indignatus*, occurring in different poems, (a) implicate Augustus, and (b) record adverse references to both acts (the sweating of statues or mention of Xerxes). Something is missing, but the construct is suggestive. For similar misgivings about *indignatum*, although without this focus, see Putnam, "Italian Virgil and the Idea of Rome", (above, n. 13) 185-187.

38. On this see J. H. D'Arms, *Romans on the Bay of Naples* (Cambridge, Mass. 1970) 40-41; he points to the Hellenistic (and luxurious) connotations of such practice. J. Griffin ("Augustan Poetry and the Life of Luxury", *JRS* 66 [1976] 90-91) makes this same connection. See too Nisbet and Hubbard (above, n. 34) 242.

39. E.g. Strabo 4.5.2; Tac. *Agr.* 12.6; *Germ.* 5.3; see also Ogilvie and Richmond 164.

40. For Horace especially, this is a pure *topos: Sat.* 1.1.41; *Odes* 1.31.6, 2.16.7-8, 2.18.1-2, 3.3.49, 3.24.48; *Epist.* 1.2.47.

41. So, for instance, Sallust views wealth as one of the chief contributors to Rome's decline (*B.C.* 7.6); on this see D. C. Earl, *The Political Thought of Sallust* (Cambridge 1961) 13-14, 42-43, 46, 70, 106, 112.

42. The attitude toward mineral wealth is covered by Schroeder 33-35; he traces the idea to the philosophers (Plato, *Rep.* 3.416 e, 4.419 a; Diogenes *ap.* Athen. 4.159 c); it was thereafter incorporated into ethnography in discussions of simple races (having also been applied in a philosophical context to early man [Plato, *Laws* 3.679 b] and the early Athenians [*Critias* 112 c]). Ethnographical instances: Anacharsis, *Epist.* 6, 10 (Scythians); Timaeus *ap.* Diodorus 5.21.6 (Britons); Trog. 2.2.7 (Scythians); Mela 2.10 (Satarchi); Val. Flacc. *Arg.* 4.131 (Arimaspi); Tac. *Germ.* 5.3.

43. There may be a similar implication at *Agr.* 12.6: *fert Britannia aurum et argentum et alia metalla, pretium victoriae ... ego facilius crediderim naturam margaritis deesse quam nobis avaritiam* (of the absence of any system in the gathering of pearls). Ogilvie and Richmond (*ad loc.*) see the first of these examples as being neutral: "These words should not be pressed to mean that Britain was invaded for the sake of these metals". I find it hard not to see some suggestion of this, however, particularly in light of the topical nature of this idea, and considering the other parallels in Tacitus. We shall return to this matter in Chapter 6.

44. In relation to this, see Schroeder 30-44 for the similarities between golden age people and those of primitive societies.

45. Pliny's account, for instance (*N.H.* 37.201), is both general and neutral: *Italia, rectrix parensque mundi altera, viris feminis, ducibus militibus, servitiis ...*

46. E.g. Caesar, *B.G.* 5.14; Sall. *B.J.* 18-19; Tac. *Agr.* 11; *Germ.* 2, 27.3. See Norden, *Die germanische Urgeschichte* 451-454 for a comprehensive catalogue of the occurrences of the title *de origine.*

47. See too Hippocrates, *aer.* 12. For this point see H. Reynen, "Ewiger Frühling" 427; I. Borzsák, "Von Hippocrates bis Vergil", in *Vergiliana*, ed. H. Bardon and R. Verdière (Leiden 1971) 41-55. That such theory was still current in Virgil's time seems clear from Livy 29.25.12: *fertilissimus ager eoque abundans omnium copia rerum est regio, et imbelles quod plerumque in uberi agro evenit, barbari sunt.* On this, see above, p. 48.

48. Reynen 427-428; Borzsák 55. Other critics (e.g. Conington, *ad loc.*) have also clearly been uneasy about the excessive emphasis on Roman militarism in Virgil's lines.

49. Servius' comment (*id est bona naturalia, non sicut in urbibus, labore quaesita, ad* 2.469) seems pointed.

50. In many ways this approximation removes the rustic from the reality of the rest of the poem (cf. above, n. 30).

51. Accordingly, Paratore (above, n. 21) 79 and others would emend; for the various candidates see Richter, apparatus and commentary, *ad loc.* Emendation, however, is not a suitable substitute for interpretation.

52. Obviously Marius is to some extent an ambivalent figure: *quanto bello optimus, tanto pace*

pessimus (Vell. 2.11.1). As far as we can tell, Livy's verdict, although also divided, seems somewhat slanted to the negative: *vir, cuius si examinentur cum virtutibus vitia, haud facile sit dictu, utrum bello melior an pace perniciosior fuerit. Adeo quam rem publicam armatus servavit, eam primo togatus omni genere fraudis, postremo armis hostiliter evertit (Per.* 80).

53. Cf. Lucr. 5.926; Cic. *leg. agr.* 2.95; Caesar, *B.G.* 6.21.3; Virg. *Geo.* 1.63; *Aen.* 5.730, 9.603; Ovid, *Trist.* 1.5.71; Lucan 2.629, 8.223; Colum. 10.137; Pliny, *N.H.* 37.203; Tac. *Ann.* 6.34; see also N. Horsfall, "Numanus Remulus: Ethnography and Propaganda in *Aen.*, ix, 598f.", *Latomus* 30 (1971) 1111.

54. Cf. Norden, *Die germanische Urgeschichte* 54, 111; also above, p. 20, below, Chapter 5.

55. This passage will be covered in Chapter 4.

56. So Reynen, "Ewiger Frühling" 427-428: "Die Bewohner Italiens sind friedliche Bauern, die ungestört ihrer Arbeit nachgehen wollen und nur, um diesen 'saturnischen' Frieden zu schützen, zur Waffe greifen, nicht weil sie von Eroberungsdrang getrieben würden". Such a reading, although very neat, finds no support from the text of Virgil's *laudes Italiae.*

57. Again I would stress, as E. Badian has indicated (above, n. 25), there seem no good reasons for denying Virgil an attitude (in this case a negative one) to the phenomenon of imperialism.

58. What appears merely on the level of a descriptive epithet here reflects a basis in ethnographical material. So for instance, Lucan's description of the Lingones (*pictis armis,* 1.398) is a poetic compression of ethnographical information which can be traced to Posidonius (Diodorus 5.30.2). For this and other such examples, see N. Pinter, *Lucanus in tradendis rebus geographicis quibus usus sit auctoribus* (diss. Münster 1902) 15ff. and *passim.* It is true that such usage becomes a part of poetic language, and may be merely ornamental, but in a passage such as the *laudes Italiae* there is justification for seeing behind this word something of the tradition which is its origin.

59. Already noted (above, n. 47); for similar theory, cf. Trog. 39.5.5; Tac. *Germ.* 12.1.

60. Contradiction and deliberate ambiguity are a part of Virgil's art; in this episode and at crucial points in the *Aeneid,* such as the exit through the gate of false dreams and the death of Turnus, he is at his most ambiguous. For this aspect of his poetry, and with reference to the two examples given, cf. J. K. Newman, *Augustus and the New Poetry,* Coll. Latomus 88 (1967) 210, 222-223, 261-269 (in effect a review of Otis); also W. V. Clausen, "An Interpretation of the *Aeneid*", *HSCP* 68 (1964) 139-147.

61. H. V. Canter, "Praise of Italy in Classical Authors", *CJ* 33 (1938) 459.

62. Otis (163) takes this word as suggesting the tree's delight. In combination with *novas,* however, the idea of surprise at an unusual or strange phenomenon (the transformation of the tree) seems predominant. This is also suggested by Servius' comment: *ingens phantasis.* Otis also appears to take *felicibus* (which he italicises) in line 81 to mean "joyful". In fact, of course, it means mainly "fruitful" or "abundant", as elsewhere in the *Georgics*: 1.54, 2.188, 4.329 (cf. Servius on the last of these: *FELICES: fertiles*).

63. Otis 163; also L. P. Wilkinson, *The Georgics of Virgil* (Cambridge 1969) 86.

64. Where they occur as real gerundives (i.e. with a sense of obligation, as opposed to milder injunctions

like *magno nunc ore sonandum, Geo.* 3.294), they are as often as not connected with battle and military force; in fact, they are mostly concentrated in the last six books of the *Aeneid*: e.g. 3.235, 5.731, 6.890 (these refer to the battles to be fought when the Trojans reach Italy), 7.444, 8.565, 566, 9.320, 10.372, 12.890.

65. E. Burck (*De Vergilii Georgicon Partibus Iussivis* [diss. Leipzig 1926] 68) has pointed out the striking arrangement of *Geo.* 2.397-419: 3 gerundives – 6 imperatives – 3 gerundives.

66. Wilkinson (above, n. 63) 86.

67. That Virgil's lines on Libya and Scythia contain ethnographical details was noted, without elaboration, by Dahlmann (549, n. 3).

68. For these details in the tradition, see Hippocrates, *aer.* 17-22; Herod. 4.28; Xen. *Anab.* 4.5.25; Mela 2.10; Tac. *Germ.* 16.4. Richter has an extensive treatment of Virgil's sources.

69. Ovid more or less appropriated these *topoi* in his descriptions of Tomis, although in this case experience doubtless contributed. For a good coverage of this tradition in poetry, see A. Cattin, "La Géographie dans les Tragédies de Sénèque", *Latomus* 22 (1963) 690-694.

70. Virgil in fact exaggerated the extent of Scythia's cold, just as he did in claiming eternal springtime for Italy. Elsewhere in the tradition there is some respite to the Scythian winter: ἔνθα τοὺς μὲν ὀκτὼ τῶν μηνῶν ἀφόρητος οἷος γίνεται κρυμός, Herod. 4.28; also Strabo 7.2.18; Varro states: *paene sempiternae hiemes, res rust.* 1.2.4; Hippocrates seems closer to Virgil: τὸν μὲν χειμῶνα ἀεὶ εἶναι (*aer.* 19), but this is mitigated by the following clause: τὸ δὲ θέρος ὀλίγας ἡμέρας καὶ ταύτας μὴ λίαν.

71. The wording in the two passages is deliberately parallel: a brief statement (*hic ver adsiduum; semper hiems*), followed by elaboration (*atque alienis mensibus aestas; semper spirantes frigora Cauri*).

72. There may be a play on the force of *tenent*, which appears in both tricolons; in the *laudes Italiae* olives and herds occupy (*tenent*) the land, while in the description of Scythia the inhabitants must keep (*tenent*) their herds in stables.

73. Notably K. Meuli, "Scythica Vergiliana, Ethnographisches, Archäologisches und Mythologisches zu Vergils Georgica 3.367ff.", *Schweiz. Archiv f. Volkskunde* 56 (1960) 91: "aber in der Schilderung der Jagd herrscht augenscheinlich eine ganz andere Stimmung: die bewundernde, froh machende Freude an einem reckenhaften, barbarisch gesunden Geschlecht, das über die Schrecken einer unüberwindlich scheinenden Umwelt zu triumphieren weiss". Meuli does not really deal with the literary aspects of the passage, since his concern is chiefly with tracing the appearance of snow-shoe hunting through various societies, ancient and modern. For the opposite view, see Otis (177-178) who elicits the greatest possible contrast, both physical and spiritual, between (for him) the totally negative environment of Scythia and that of the Italian spring.

74. *Geo.* 2.468 is curious in that Virgil later used the first part of it to describe the city of Carthage: *dives opum studiisque asperrima belli, Aen.* 1.14. *Bellum* has replaced *otium*, its opposite. In the passage from the Second Georgic, however, the phrase *dives opum* has a somewhat different sense to it.

75. There are no grounds for assuming, as Otis did (178), a moral condemnation of beer-drinking; rather this is evidence of their ability to overcome the restrictions of their surroundings (*neque ullae ... aut arbore frondes*, 3.352-352). In the ethnographical tradition there is no hint of the pejorative in such

activity; the detail appears as early as Hecataeus of Miletus (*ap.* Athen. 10. 447 d = *FGH* 1 fr. 154); also Pytheas of Massilia *ap.* Strabo 4.5.5; Tac. *Germ.* 22-23.

76. Again, see Schroeder (35-45) for similarities between barbarian and Utopian societies.

77. Horace was to reiterate his view later in the poem:

> vel nos in mare proximum
> gemmas et lapides, aurum et inutile
> summi materiem mali,
> mittamus.
>
> (47-50)

78. So they appear in Hippocrates, *aer.* 18; Herod. 4.2; Aesch. *Prom.* 709; Sallust, *Hist.* 3 fr. 76 M. For this as a *topos* of ethnography, see Schroeder 18-21. Virgil made the Libyans nomadic (which is also traditional; Strabo 17.3.1; Richter *ad Geo.* 3.339ff.) and the Scythians sedentary.

79. Cf. Caesar, *B.G.* 4.1, of the Suebi; Tac. *Germ.* 26.1-2. Caesar's Suebi are, in fact, very much like Virgil's Scythians: they live by hunting rather than organized agriculture, are free of societal duties, and dress in animal skins.

80. This moralistic stance became a more integral part of later ethnography, particularly in the *Germania*, where Tacitus suggests (as Horace stated) that the examples of primitive societies should be followed by the Romans, who had lost their more admirable and traditional moral qualities. On this, see below, Chapter 6.

81. The adjective is only used one other time in a personal sense by Horace, in *Epistles* 1.1, while talking of his own ethical stance in those poems: *virtutis verae custos rigidusque satelles*, 17.

82. *Liber* in this context implies both spontaneity of growth and perhaps common ownership, both Saturnian features.

83. Here the description of Libya (3.339-348) may be briefly dealt with. We have already referred to its lack of formal development and comparative brevity (above, n. 11) – although the diction is still ethnographical: *mapalia* (340), for instance, which appears here for the first time in poetry, was used by Sallust in his ethnographical survey of Libya (*B.J.* 18.8). But what of meaning of the passage? I believe it has, in microcosm, the same function as the Scythian episode. In the extremity of its heat it is clearly to be seen as a negative setting. And yet, just as Scythia was to some extent redeemed, so Virgil obliquely suggests that all is not wrong with Libya. Among the Africans' belongings are the following: *armaque Amyclaeumque canem Cressamque pharetram*, 345. Spartan hounds and Cretan quiver; what, we may ask (and critics have asked), has the Libyan to do with such items? Richter's suggestion of Nicander, *Theriaca* 670 makes no sense in context, particularly since this line refers only to the dogs. The one common feature of the Spartans and the Cretans is their well-organized constitution: *quem enim oratorem Lacedaemonium, quem Cretensem accepimus?* asks Tacitus' Maternus (*Dial.* 40-3; cf. Gudeman *ad loc.*), implying of course, that the well-organized and harmonious state has no place for oratory. Schroeder has shown (51-52) that Sparta and Crete were regarded in the ethnographical tradition as paradigms for the ideal state, disdaining, among other things, organized agriculture and the use of gold and silver. I suggest, then, that at *Geo.* 3.345 Virgil has, by reference to Sparta and Crete (this is the only connection between the two societies, and it is a *topos*), suggested that the Libyan (like the Scythian) is not totally flawed; redemption comes through assigning qualities which once again create a deliberate contrast to the civilized society of the *laudes Italiae.*

84. So Otis, Wilkinson (above, n. 63), Paratore (above, n. 21), Klingner (above, n. 3) and Putnam (above, n. 13) devote no more than two pages each to this episode. J. Perret (*Virgile, l'homme et l'oeuvre* [Paris 1952] 70) does see the structural importance of the passage (parallel in position and related in theme to the description of the passing of the golden age, 1.125-146), but his treatment goes no further than this. A notable exception is E. Burck's "Der korykische Greis in Vergils Georgica", *Navicula Chilonensis* (Leiden 1956) 156-172 (= *Vom Menschenbild in der Römischen Literatur* [Heidelberg 1966] 117-129). It is perhaps interesting that in this article, published some thirty years after his "Die Komposition von Vergils Georgika", (above, n. 2), Burck greatly modified his earlier claim that all parts of the poem must be given equal attention. Of some value is P. Wuilleumier's "Virgile et le Vieillard de Tarente", *REL* 8 (1930) 325-340; this is somewhat flawed by a biographical, or historical approach to Virgil's poem.

85. E.g. Cato, *agr. cult* 8.2; Varro, *res rust.* 1.16.3. See Burck (above, n. 84) 163ff. for the basic difference in tone between Virgil and his technical predecessors, whose concern is with the commercial utility of market-gardens (*fundi suburbani*), particularly in supplying the city markets.

86. Burck (above, n. 84), 167, n. 2, suggests a parallel with *Geo.* 2.155-157, but those lines are to be distinguished (as we have indicated, above, pp. 41-2) in that they emphasize the artificial, man-made features which have been imposed on the natural setting.

87. See Richter *ad loc.* for bibliographical details; he prefers a less specific answer: the basic Roman farmer. This, however, gives no help in explaining why *Corycium*?

88. Virgil himself, as we shall see (below in Chapter 4), included such a section when drawing from the tradition in the Eighth Aeneid.

89. Cf. above, Introduction, p. 3, and above, n. 46.

90. Particularly in the *laudes Italiae*, where he catalogued some of the original components of the Roman state: Marsians, Sabines, Ligurians, Volsci (2.167-168).

91. Richter notes at this point, without elaboration, and without reference to the parallel lines in the *laudes Italiae* and the depiction of Scythia, that the categories are those of Books 3, 1 and 2.

92. See Burck (above, n. 84) 158-159 for a clear discussion of Virgil's emphasis on the old man's self-sufficiency.

93. If this line has a bearing on the theme we have traced, it is quite possible that Virgil's choice of this verb is pointed.

94. Cf. Burck (above, n. 84) 169 for notice of this parallel.

95. A further parallel from Horace's poetry should be mentioned; at the beginning of *Odes* 2.15 he referred to man's assault on nature:

> iam *pauca* aratro *iugera* regiae
> moles *relinquent*, undique latius
>   extenta visentur Lucrino
>   stagna lacu.
>   (1-4)

The works of man are taking over the entire landscape, with *piscinae* opening on all sides. There is here a possible reminiscence both of the old man's plot (*cui* pauca relicti/iugera *ruris erant, Geo.* 4.127-128) and of the position of the Lucrine in the *laudes Italiae*.

96. As has already been suggested (above, n. 30), success in the *Georgics* which is in terms of golden age settings is to be distinguished. That age Virgil specifically excluded from the real, georgic world (1.125-149).

97. As an alternative to Tibur, which seems to represent his own, specifically Horatian poetic landscape (see above, p. 60).

98. The lines have not eluded the imagination of critics; Munro supposed that the *Eclogues* were written at Tarentum, Wuilleumier (above, n. 116, 332) that the final draft was produced there, either at the conclusion of a trip from Metapontum (subsequently confused by Servius as the voyage on which Virgil died), or following the journey to Brundisium described by Horace in *Satires* 1.5!

99. Noted by P. J. Enk (*Sex. Propertii Elegiarum Liber Secundus* [Leiden 1961]) on Prop. 2.34.67.

100. By Wuilleumier (above, n. 30) 327. For the appropriateness of the Galaesus to a pastoral setting, see M. Rothstein, *Die Elegien des Sextus Propertius* I (Berlin 1898) *ad* 2.34.67.

101. Taken in this way, it is much the same as Propertius' water imagery: *non ego velifera tumidum mare findo carina:/tota sub* exiguo *flumine nostra mora est*, 3.9.35-36; cf. also 4.1.59; Ovid, *Fast.* 2.4, 6.22.

102. See Ross (above, n. 30) 76 on Prop. 1.11.9-12, where the diminutive *parvula* appears in company with *tenuis*, both with programmatic force.

103. For a good examination of the end of *Odes* 2.16 in terms of its place in the poetics of Roman poetry, see Ross (above, n. 30) 132, n. 1, 148.

104. Burck (above, n. 84) 169-170.

III. OF BEES, ORPHEUS AND MEN: THE FOURTH *GEORGIC*

The problem with the Fourth Georgic (and it is a problem which ultimately affects the entire poem) rests in the relationship of the second half – the epyllion on Orpheus – to the first – the description of the bees' society.[1] The present chapter will examine this description, then offer an explanation of the whole book in connection with the themes which have so far been traced in the *Georgics*.

Dahlmann's claim that Virgil drew extensively from the ethnographical tradition when depicting the bees' society[2] has attracted such opposition that it is now mentioned mainly in passing.[3] From the last chapter it should be clear that such influence is at least possible; as we proceed, support for Dahlmann's view will emerge. At the same time, however, some of the flaws in his interpretation of the ethnographic depiction (and these have tended to obscure the real merits of his identification) should also become apparent.

The description in the Fourth Georgic, unlike those with which we have been dealing, lacks a neatness of form; all the categories are present, but the conciseness and order, by now familiar in this tradition, are lacking. This in fact reflects a division in the genre apparent in prose ethnography. The abbreviated version, whose focus is predominantly on the physical features of the land, its climate and its produce, and which is more purely descriptive than expansive, is the type which has thus far appeared.[4] In addition there is a more extended type of study whose concerns are less with physical detail and more with the *mores* and institutions of the inhabitants.[5] As is apparent from Dahlmann's categories,[6] it is this type which provided Virgil with his model. The reason for such a distinction in terms of the *Georgics* is clear. A fully developed ethnographical description of Scythia, for instance, along the lines of Herodotus' version, would be inappropriate. It is, however, poetically acceptable to describe a non-human society through a genre traditionally reserved for descriptions of human societies.

This leads to what should be an obvious point: the fact that the bee world is presented in the form of an ethnography compels us to view their society as in some way analogous to, and symbolic of, a human one. They must represent a human society (precisely what type will emerge below). It is, therefore, rather surprising to read such statements as: "It [the Fourth Georgic] is about bees before it is about anything else".[7] Technical authors such as Aristotle or Varro may be primarily concerned with bees as bees, but if we claim the same for Virgil, we will not begin to understand his poem. Klingner, dealing with the poem as a whole, has put it well: "der Dichter spricht nur, *als ob* er Landwirtschaft lehre".[8] It should be our task to detect what stands behind the metaphor.

To begin with, it will be of use to examine any sources which may have suggested to Virgil the potential for such a means of description. From observation of the bees' communal life, of course, the general comparison with man is quite a natural one, and, as has been noted, both Cicero (*de off.* 1.157) and Varro (*res rust.* 3.16.4, 6, 9, 29, 30)[9] had commented on the similarity. There may, in fact, have been a direct source for Virgil within the tradition of apicultural writing; a few years before the *Georgics* were written, Varro, dealing with the same topic, purely from the technical standpoint, advised the following:

> primum secundum villam potissimum, ubi non resonant imagines (hic enim sonus harum fugae existimatur esse protelum), esse oportet aere temperato, neque aestate fervido neque hieme non aprico, ut spectet potissimum ad hibernos ortus, qui prope se loca habeat ea, ubi pabulum sit frequens et aqua pura, si pabulum naturale non est, ea oportet dominum serere, quae maxima secuntur apes.
>
> (*res rust.* 3.16.12-13)

Situs, climatic conditions and food-supply are all covered. The terminology, moreover, is that which appears in ethnography (cf. *aere temperato*; *ut spectet potissimum ad hibernos ortus*). The seeds, then, of an ethnographical treatment are already in the technical tradition.[10] It seems plausible that Virgil, who certainly read Varro's treatise, could have seen in this account the potential for a fully developed ethnographical description, which would balance the briefer versions elsewhere in the poem.

In fact, Varro's entire section on the bees already contains the basis for much of Virgil's material. Again applying Dahlmann's *topoi* we can see the treatment of environment (περὶ τόπων) in Varro's account (3.16.12, 15, 23). Also present are: εἶδος and ἰσχύς (3.16.18, 19), ὅπλισις and τρόπος τῆς μάχης (3.16.7, 9, 30), organization of *res domesticae* (3.16.4), *praedivinatio* (3.16.37), and, finally, on kings and rulers (3.16.6, 8, 18). That is, the only categories which have no counterpart in Varro's version are the τόπος περὶ ταφῆς and ἴδια καὶ παράδοξα. It should be noted, however, that the parallel passages in his treatise are scattered throughout the work, and there is no real impression of a systematic ethnographical treatment.

The material, then, was in essence already in the tradition of the technical writers. Virgil saw the potential and, on one level, mainly through arrangement, transformed the subject so as to produce an approximation to human society.[11] He strengthened this approximation by stating in open terms what had previously been expressed through simile. To Varro the swarming of the bees had seemed like the sending out of a colony (*cum ... progeniem ut coloniam emittere volunt, ut olim crebro Sabini factitaverunt, res rust.* 3.16.29); just before they swarm they seem like soldiers in a camp (3.16.30); they work and build like man (3.16.4); the organization of their life is similar to that of an army (3.16.9); in short, their whole society is like man's (*haec ut hominum civitates, quod hic est et rex et imperium et societas*, 3.16.6). And what of Virgil? With one exception (*vox/auditur fractos sonitus imitata tubarum*, 4.71-72; cf. *ut imitatione tubae, res rust.* 3.16.9) – rather a necessary exception – Virgil completely removed the similes and comparisons, and simply described the bees' activities as if they were those of men.

Even more significantly, Virgil occasionally suppressed details which would align his subject with the world of bees rather than men. It is surely not accidental that he fails to note in the battle scene (67-87) that this is in fact a swarming rather than a battle (as for instance Varro did; *res rust.* 3.16.30). Throughout the description, moreover, as Dahlmann noted, Virgil has applied to the bees terminology normally reserved for description of the world of men.[12] And finally he has falsely claimed that the bees are unique in some of their more human-like activities: "*Solae* (153, 155) overlooks the wasp and the ant, that proverbial hoarder for the winter".[13] Indeed this is no oversight, but rather a deliberate contradiction, not only of established entomology, but even of information occurring elsewhere in the *Georgics*:

> curculio atque inopi metuens formica senectae.
>
> (1.186)

So important is it for Virgil in the Fourth Georgic to make the bees (and only the bees) analogous to men.

The next question is how far such symbolism can be carried; or rather, are we dealing with allegory? L. Herrmann and J. Perret saw in the bees a symbol for the participants of Actium.[14] This view, based for the most part on an epigram of Philip of Thessalonica (*Anth. Pal.* 6.236), is far too specific to fit most of the details of the description. It was in any case superseded by the theory of Dahlmann, who, after identifying the depiction of the bees' society as an ethnographical description, proceeded to claim that it was intended as a paradigm, an example of right action to be followed by the Roman people. He too then claimed (559-562) that it was a specifically historical symbolism ("wo das vordergründig Ausgesprochene letzlich nur als Gleichnis dient", 560); accordingly the good king is a representation of Octavian, the bad one of Antony. The war between these kings stands for civil war, with the triumph of Octavian representing the legitimization, in terms of natural law, of the new regime. So, what Seneca expressed directly in his justification of Nero's natural right to rule (*de clem.* 1.19), Virgil stated "in hintergründiger Symbolik" (561).

L. P. Wilkinson[15] has indicated some of the inconsistencies and difficulties in Dahlmann's final conclusions. The replacement of the family by a communistic society (153-157)[16] and the total absence of sexual communion are hardly in line with future Augustan policy. While the word *Quirites* (201) may suggest the people of Rome (although it need mean little more than "citizens"), and while the good leader (90-93) may suggest Octavian, as the bad one (93-94) suggests Antony, such a fabric becomes intolerable (as a piece of Augustan propaganda) when Virgil proceeds to advise, a few lines later, as the best way of preventing swarming:

> tu regibus alas
eripe.
>
> (106-107)

In this connection we should also be aware of the fact that the distinction between good and bad rulers was already a part of the technical tradition before the writing of the *Georgics* (*duo, niger et varius, qui ita melior, ut expediat mellario, cum duo sint in eadem alvo, interficere nigrum, cum sit cum altero rege, esse seditiosum et corrumpere alvom*, Varro, *res rust.* 3.16.18). The language of civil strife, then, is a part of the tradition received by Virgil.

Beyond these seemingly insurmountable objections, there are more general logical inconsistencies in an allegorical reading of this part of the poem. For if Octavian is represented by the king-bee, then who throws the dust to settle their quarrel (86-87)? Who, moreover, is Aristaeus, and who Proteus? All of these have a greater power over the bee community than does the king, and yet, with the exception of Proteus, none is in a position of divinity.

Dahlmann also implies (551) that the descriptive terms used by Virgil (e.g. *lares, penates, patria*, etc.) suggest a specifically Roman context. While this is possible, it is not necessary; for, as we have seen (above, n. 12), such words are also used in describing the rest of the animal world. What is more, terms which are used to describe traditionally Roman institutions are found elsewhere in Virgil's poetry in application to people with no connection with Rome.[17]

In short, a strict interpretation of Virgil's account of the bees' society as an historical allegory ultimately fails; while there is clearly an approximation of their society to that of man, their society should not be made to represent an historical moment in the experience of the Roman people.

We should also be wary of reading Virgil through the eyes of Seneca (so Dahlmann 547-548, 559, 561-562).[18] Seneca was concerned with providing a justification of monarchy; he therefore took Virgil's account of the king-bees (he could as effectively have used Varro's treatise) and applied it for his own purposes in relation to Nero. To impute to Virgil the same intention in the *Georgics* is unjustified. At this point, moreover, the concept of a *rex* was still particularly abhorrent, and to use it even as a symbolic title for Octavian would have been as unthinkable for Virgil as it would be embarrassing for Octavian.[19] Also the emphasis in Seneca's section is on the services and benefits provided by the king. For Virgil this aspect is minimal, and is only briefly mentioned (*ille operum custos*, 215). Surely if the point were glorification of a new *rex* Virgil too would have stressed this quality. So, while Seneca may have seen the potential for allegory, that is no support for seeing in Virgil's lines the same intention.

What, then, is the nature and purpose of the ethnographical depiction of the

Fourth Georgic? We have already suggested that it contributes to an overall compositional balance gained by Virgil's separating of the first three books into the three agricultural categories of the ethnographical tradition, and then presenting the actual technical material of the fourth book as an ethnographical study (above, pp. 35-6). But this is only the compositional framework.

The nature of the ethnographical information in the Fourth Georgic is not always easy to recover. Their communal housing and sharing of offspring (153) are traditionally features of less advanced societies, as is their collective attitude towards their produce (*in medium quaesita reponunt*, 157 – this is, of course, also a feature of the golden age, *in medium quaerebant, Geo.* 1.127). Their contempt of death (84-85, 203-204, 236-238) is also consistent with an ethnographical *topos* applied to simple, uncivilized societies.[20] Yet these are also features demanded by observation of the bees' society, and it is, I think, erroneous to claim, on the basis of such detail, that they represent, for instance, "a simple folk living ideally close to nature".[21] For in the very same lines the bees are governed by laws (*magnis agitant sub legibus aevum*, 154), which are alien to the golden age (Ovid, *Met.* 1.90), and not much in evidence in primitive societies. The specified absence of sexual communion, moreover (197-199), is hardly consistent with the promiscuity which usually attends the sharing of children in less advanced societies.[22]

To some extent, then, the world of the bees is a mélange; it seems that Virgil's intention is in many ways to approximate their society to that of man. Yet there does seem to be one consistent and predominant stance, and one which relates closely to the rest of the *Georgics* – the emphasis on the bees' devotion and subjection to *labor*. In this characteristic, which separates them from the world of simple society,[23] they are inextricably tied to the age of Jupiter as defined by Virgil himself (*Geo.* 1.125-146). This feature, together with their innate love of possession (*innatus apes amor urget habendi*, 127), is ultimately the chief motivating force of their world, and the one which defines their relationship to the other cultural levels of the poem.

The post-Saturnian *labor*[24] which Jupiter imposed on man in the First Georgic is the very essence of the bees' society. Their world is specified as belonging to this later age:

> nunc age, naturas apibus quas Iuppiter ipse
> addidit expediam.

(4.149-150)

Although this also refers to Jupiter's rewarding of the bees for their earlier services to him,[25] it is difficult to avoid seeing a reference to the addition, also by Jupiter,[26] of one of the post-golden age elements in the first book of the poem:

> ille malum virus serpentibus addidit atris.

(129)

The form *addidit* is used in the *Georgics* only in these two places; also of possible significance is another line from the same context (*mox et frumentis* labor additus, 1.150). The world of the bees is one of *experientia* (1.4) and *ars* (4.56), virtually synonymous qualities (as is clear from *Geo.* 4.315-316: *quis deus hanc, Musae, quis nobis extudit artem?/ unde nova ingressus hominum experientia cepit?), the latter of which is specified as a mark of the world after Saturn (1.122, 133, 145).*

   But it is chiefly in his emphasis on the bees' labor that Virgil establishes the cultural stage of their society; this comes mainly in the verses treating their social institutions and organization (149ff.). He stresses the division and intensity of their work (158-169), which was covered briefly by Aristotle (*hist. anim.* 9.40 625b 17ff.), by Varro not at all. In these lines, and elsewhere, it is the communal aspect of their *labor* which Virgil presented as their salient characteristic:

>   omnibus una quies operum, labor omnibus unus.
>   (184)[27]

The entire hive is occupied throughout the day and into the night:

>   mane ruunt portis, nusquam mora; rursus easdem
>   Vesper ubi e pastu tandem decedere campis
>   admonuit, tum tecta petunt, tum corpora curant;
>   (185-187)
>   at fessae multa referunt se nocte minores.
>   (180)[28]

Bees, as Wilkinson has noted, "do not return late at night" (p. 265). Again, fact is altered to support a view of incessant toil. This *labor* is so much the motivating force that it is pursued by the bees even at the expense of their individual lives:

>   saepe etiam duris errando in cotibus alas
>   attrivere, ultroque animam sub fasce dedere:
>   tantus amor florum et generandi gloria mellis.
>   (203-205)

The final line of this passage refers back to an earlier one, also related to the motivation for the bees' toil; after comparing their work to that of the Cyclopes (170-175), Virgil remarks:

>   non aliter, si parva licet componere magnis,
>   Cecropias innatus apes amor urget habendi
>   munere quamque suo.
>   (176-178)

Amor habendi – the love of possession. The phrase was to become a virtual formula in descriptions of the inferior ages which follow the fall of Saturn; in *Aeneid* 8 Evander claims of the degeneration which set in after the golden age:

> sic placida populos in pace regebat
> deterior donec paulatim ac decolor aetas
> et belli rabies et *amor* successit *habendi.*
>   (*Aen.* 8.325-327)[29]

This same feature characterizes Ovid's bronze age, with the negativity strengthened by the pejorative epithet, *sceleratus:*

> in quorum subiere locum fraudesque dolusque
> insidiaeque et vis et *amor sceleratus habendi.*
>   (*Met.* 1.130-131)

This feature of the bees' society, then, which is the single most motivating force in their world, sets them unequivocally on the level of an advanced, latter-day civilization. Their world is at odds with the moderate self-sufficiency of the old man of Tarentum, and it is at the same time incompatible with the Saturnian setting of Virgil's idealized rustic at the end of the second book – indeed it seems explicitly so:

> neque ille
> aut doluit miserans inopem aut *invidit habenti.*
>   (2.498-499)

Also in its lack of *otium* the bees' culture seems deliberately to contrast with that of the rustic (2.498, 523-531). In general, as was the case with the *laudes Italiae,* so here there seems to be a conscious opposition between the bees and the rustic.[30] In terms of the stages of cultural development which Virgil defines and applies throughout the *Georgics,* the society of the bees is a paradigm for the extent to which *labor,* the chief characteristic of advanced civilization, can permeate a culture.

Before examining Virgil's attitude to this society, that is his view of its ability to succeed as well as his view of its desirability, we should perhaps recapitulate. In books 1 and 3 of the *Georgics,* as is normally agreed, Virgil presented the world of civilized *labor,* as it exists in the area of agriculture. That world was swept away, powerless against the forces of nature; the *labor* expended by man was ultimately fallible. In the Fourth Georgic, Virgil has presented us with a society which, through the device of ethnography, is a virtual paradigm for human society; this culture, moreover, is one which also demonstrates a propensity towards the values of *labor.* It will be our argument that Virgil has here implicated man, that is civilized, *labor*-oriented man, in the complex of Books 1 and 3 – his judgement of the bees' society will stand as his judgement of the human society which operates with such values.

In pursuing this question, once again we shall consider important Virgil's departures from traditional material. Such departures are often ascribed to error or misunderstanding (e.g. by Conington or Wilkinson), but it is, I think, preferable, at least at the outset, to consider the poetic function of such "errors"; only if these details are purely gratuitous should we discount them as mistakes. I shall also argue that Virgil portrays the bees' world as being as susceptible to disaster as the rest of his organized world. By conveying that susceptibility on an allusive level, he undercuts his more obvious and straightforward remarks, such as his suggestion of the bees' immortality:[31]

> at genus immortale manet, multosque per annos
> stat fortuna domus, et avi numerantur avorum.
>
> (208-209)

As with the *laudes Italiae*, so here, it will emerge that Virgil's more blatant claims are at variance with implications which are to be drawn from a deeper, more allusive level of expression.

To begin with, we should return to the ethnographical category which is the setting for Virgil's description of the bees, their *situs*.[32] His primary concern is to emphasize the hazards which exist for the bees; in doing this Virgil equates their world to that of the livestock in the third book. And the fate of that world in the *Georgics* is all too apparent. First, the hives are to be sheltered from the wind: *quo neque sit ventis aditus*, 9. This recalls Virgil's precepts for the housing of livestock: *iubeo ...|et stabula a ventis hiberno opponere soli| ad medium conversa diem*, 3.300-303. In Book 4 the statement is consistent with Hippocratic theory (and therefore at home in the context of ethnographical *situs*) in that the effects of wind-exposure are there emphasized.[33] Yet it is also modified to suit the context of apiary description (*nam pabula venti|ferre domum prohibent* 9-10). Such detail, moreover, seems to be outside the technical tradition.[34] Significantly, then, in the very first lines of the depiction, Virgil has introduced an element which emphasizes the precarious nature of the bees' community, and in doing so has drawn a parallel with previously treated animals whose community eventually crumbled because of its susceptibility to such natural phenomena.

Certain destructive elements threaten the bees, and must be kept away:

> neque oves haedique petulci
> floribus insultent, aut errans bucula campo
> decutiat rorem et surgentis atterat herbas.
> absint et picti squalentia terga lacerti
> pinguibus a stabulis, meropesque aliaeque volucres
> et manibus Procne pectus signata cruentis;
> omnia nam late vastant ipsasque volantis
> ore ferunt dulcem nidis immitibus escam.
>
> (10-17)

Just so, in the first book, the crops, the product of man's *labor*, were threatened as they lay on the threshing floor:

ne subeant herbae neu pulvere victa fatiscat,
tum variae inludant pestes: saepe exiguus mus
sub terris posuitque domos atque horrea fecit,
aut oculis capti fodere cubilia talpae,
inventusque cavis bufo et quae plurima terrae
monstra ferunt, populatque ingentem farris acervum
curculio atque inopi metuens formica senectae.

(1.180-186)[35]

So too, in the third book, thorny shrubs represent a hindrance in the breeding of sheep for wool (*si tibi lanitium curae, primum aspera silva/lappaeque tribolique absint*, 3.384-385). It seems significant that Virgil only twice used the verb *absint*, here, and in the related passage at 4.13. Later in the third book (414-439), Virgil dwells at length on the threat of snakes[36] (*pestis acerba boum*, 419),[37] in a passage, moreover, immediately preceding the onset of the plague. In short, then, at the very beginning of describing the bees' habitat, Virgil emphasized the threats to which these creatures are exposed; in doing so, moreover, he aligned their environment with those of Books 1 and 3, worlds of *labor* which eventually fell in spite of man's efforts to preserve them. A final point: at line 15 (and again at 191) the bee-hive is called *stabulum*; these are the only two instances of the word applied to housing other than that of larger animals.

Virgil then proceeded to treat the positive side of the setting (*adsint*, 19). Most of the details are traditional (see Conington *ad* 4.18), but after prescribing the general environment, he stated:

in medium, seu stabit iners seu profluet umor,
transversas salices et grandia conice saxa,
pontibus ut crebris possint consistere et alas
pandere ad aestivum solem, si forte morantis
sparserit aut praeceps Neptuno immerserit Eurus.

(4.25-29)

Here Virgil has deliberately altered the tradition. He gives as the reason for placing stones in pools their need to rest (*ut ... possint consistere*). As observation of bees shows, and as Varro (whom, again, Virgil will have read) states (*ut bibere possint, res rust.* 3.16.27), the bees actually take in water.[38] Virgil's explanation appears to be a deliberate substitution for that of Varro, an explanation found elsewhere only in Columella (9.5.5.), who cited Virgil and through his admiration for the poet was at this point blind to the tradition. Why, then, Virgil's departure from the traditional material? By suppressing the real reason Virgil has created yet another danger to which the bee society is susceptible – the threat of storms (*praeceps Neptuno immerserit Eurus*, 29). Again, in precisely the same way, the crops of the first book were swept away by the autumn and spring storms (*ruit arduus aether/et pluvia ingenti sata laeta boumque* labores/*diluit*, 1.324-326). So too the sheep-fold of the Third Georgic (which likewise needs a supply of water: *fluvios ... recentis*, 301) is subject to the threat of storms: *cum frigidus olim/iam cadit extremoque inrorat Aquarius anno*, 303-304.

As a sub-category of *situs*, Virgil treated the construction of the hive; whatever you use to make these, you should ensure that the entrances are narrow:

> nam frigore mella
> cogit hiems, eademque calor liquefacta remittit.
> utraque vis apibus pariter metuenda.
> (35-37)

As Aristotle had pointed out, the bees make the entrances of their hives narrow in order to exclude intruders (*hist. anim.* 9.40 623b 30). Only Columella (9.7.4)[39] gives temperature as a reason for this feature, and, as has been noted (by Conington, *ad* 4.35), this is probably in deference to Virgil (Columella in fact even questions the actual damage caused by heat: *nec tamen ita nocet huic generi calor aestatis ut hiemale frigus*, 9.7.4).[40] In Virgil's eyes no factor is greater in restricting the advance or threatening the survival of man than extreme heat or cold. This much was obvious in his description of Scythia, and in the symptoms of destructive *amor* and the plague in the third book. Once again, his introduction of this theme as a consideration in the building of the hive demonstrates his concern to present, through the bees, a society which is fragile in the face of these the most dangerous and destructive of nature's forces.

At this point Virgil has provided the reader with a significant footnote:

> utraque vis apibus pariter metuenda.
> (4.37)

Of the eight instances of the verb *metuo* in the *Georgics*, six refer to that fear which results from the inability to control the elements or some other feature of the natural world.[41] Storms, untimely showers and extremes of temperature are all components of the world of *labor*, and it is man's inability to overcome these which makes him forever susceptible to fear. So the bees. Ovid seems to have been aware of this when, in his description of the golden age, he specifically excluded *metus* from that world (*poena metusque aberant, Met.* 1.91). It is perhaps also to the point that Virgil himself, in the middle of describing the idealized, and in many ways Saturnian, rustic at the end of the Second Georgic, should have proclaimed:

> felix qui potuit rerum cognoscere causas
> atque *metus* omnis et inexorabile fatum
> subiecit pedibus strepitumque Acherontis avari.
> (2.490-492)

I certainly find no such victory in the technical or "didactic" parts of the poem, and most of all not in the world of the bees, which, in its susceptibility to such *metus*, as in other respects, is firmly identified with the post-Saturnian, *labor*-oriented era.

Having dealt with insulation, Virgil proceeded to the bees' occupation of underground caverns:

> saepe etiam effossis, si vera est fama, latebris
> sub terra fovere larem, penitusque repertae
> pumicibusque cavis exesaeque arboris antro.
>   (42-44)

The information seems gratuitous, and is surely of little value to the bee-keeper. And yet, in terms of the ethnographical theme of the *Georgics*, it is highly relevant; for we will recall the living conditions of the Scythians:

> ipsi in defossis specubus secura sub alta
> otia agunt terra, congestaque robora totasque
> advolvere focis ulmos ignique dedere.
>   (3.376-378)[42]

The similarities (cf. *effossis/defossis*) strengthen the approximation of the bees to men, and, more than this, as with the Scythians, so too with the bees, there is a suggestion of fragility, in that both societies are compelled to live beneath the earth as a protection against an adverse environment. A further point: the phrase *si vera fama est* (4.42), as was the case with Horace's *si credis* (Epist. 1.16.15),[43] is appropriate to this detail of the bees' *situs*; for the lines effectively constitute an ethnographical *thaumasion*.

Virgil completes his requirements for the bees' habitat with yet another veto (45-50): there should be no yew trees in the area, no burning crab-shells,[44] no marshes, and, finally, their hives should not be exposed to echoes. Throughout the description of their setting, then, even to the extent of altering the tradition, Virgil stressed the hazards to which these creatures are subject; the final impression is one of the bees' susceptibility.

The natural question at this point is whether and how this impression is realized elsewhere in the account of the bees' society. The basis for examining this will be in the parallels which Virgil suggests between their world and that of the smaller animals in the second half of the third book (284-566). It will be our suggestion that the fate of those animals is also the fate of the bees, and through them that of civilized society in general.

It should be noted at the outset that there are compositional parallels which invite comparison of these two sequences. At 3.286 Virgil, as he turned to his new theme, noted: *superat pars altera curae*. Although this refers chiefly to the division of the third book, it in some ways anticipates the opening of the fourth: *hanc etiam, Maecenas, aspice partem* (4.2).[45] These, incidentally, are the only two instances in the *Georgics* of the word *pars* in this concrete sense. But an even more striking parallel is in the chiastic structure of the opening proem of each section. At 3.284-297 Virgil claimed that the narrowness of his subject (*angustis ... rebus*, 290) would be compensated for by elevation of style (*magno nunc ore sonandum*, 294); in the opening of the fourth book, lofty subject matter (*magnanimosque duces totiusque ordine gentis/mores et studia et populos et proelia dicam*, 4-5) will be mitigated by slight manner (*in tenui labor*, 6).[46]

Let us look now to the content of the two sections. At the beginning, in both, Virgil dealt with steading (*incipiens stabulis ...* 3.295; *principio sedes*, 4.8). As we saw with the bees, so too for the sheep, sufficient insulation is required (*glacies ne frigida laedat/molle pecus scabiemque ferat turpisque podagras*, 3.298-299).[47] Again, the threat against these creatures, as for the bees, is expressed in terms of climatic extremes. In discussing the ideal environment for animals, as was the case with the negative setting, there are further parallels: goats are to be surrounded by foliage (*frondentia ... arbuta*, 3.300-301), with water nearby, and sheltered from the wind (3.300-304) – details which also occur in the recommended habitat of the bees (4.9, 23-29; cf. *hospitiis frondentibus*).

In both books, after these sections, Virgil treated the springtime emergence of the animals and the bees:

> at vero Zephyris cum laeta vocantibus aestas
> in saltus utrumque gregem atque in pascua mittet,
> Luciferi primo cum sidere frigida rura
> carpamus, dum mane novum, dum gramina canent,
> et ros in tenera pecori gratissimus herba.
>
> (3.322-326)
>
> quod superest, ubi pulsam hiemem sol aureus egit
> sub terras caelumque aestiva luce reclusit,
> illae continuo saltus silvasque peragrant
> purpureosque metunt flores et flumina libant
> summa leves.
>
> (4.51-55)

The orchestration is the same in both passages: after surviving the winter, the animals and bees issue forth and enjoy the spring and summer pastures (*saltus*, 3.323, 4.53). Again, Virgil seems to be suggesting a connection between the two groups. Also in the third book, while dealing with the production of wool, Virgil stated that breeding must be pure:

> illum autem, quamvis aries sit candidus ipse,
> nigra subest udo tantum cui lingua palato,
> reice, ne maculis infuscet vellera pullis
> nascentum.
>
> (3.387-390)

The same weeding-out process must be carried out with leaders of the hive:

> deterior qui visus, eum, ne prodigus obsit,
> dede neci; melior vacua sine regnet in aula.
> alter erit maculis auro squalentibus ardens –
> (4.89-91)

In both cases the distinction can be made by colour (cf. *maculis*, 3.389, 4.91); Virgil's tone of urgency, moreover, is the same in both passages (*reice*; *dede neci*).

To this point, then, there are a number of indications that Virgil intended his readers to see the two sequences as in some ways parallel. The chief similarity, and the one which gives meaning to the whole complex, lies in the onset of illness and plague, which occurs in both environments.[48] In each case, advice to fumigate against *pestes* (*disce et odoratum stabulis accendere cedrum/galbaneoque agitare gravis nidore chelydros*, etc. 3.414ff.; *at suffire thymo cerasque recidere inanis/quis dubitet? nam saepe favos ignotus adedit/stelio*, 4.241ff.),[49] leads into treatment of the symptoms of the illness (3.440ff.; 4.251ff.), and finally, in both instances, Virgil closes with a totally destructive plague.

In its general movement, this seems to be indebted to Lucretius' account of the plague in the sixth book of the *De Rerum Natura* (1090-1286); the following pattern emerges:

General symptoms:

> nunc ratio quae sit morbis aut unde repente
> mortiferam possit cladem conflare coorta
> morbida vis hominum generi pecudumque catervis
> expediam.
> > (Lucr. 6.1090-1093)
> morborum quoque te causas et signa docebo.
> > (*Geo.* 3.440)
> si vero, quoniam casus apibus quoque nostros
> vita tulit, tristi languebant corpora morbo –
> quod iam non dubiis poteris cognoscere signis:
> > (*Geo.* 4.251-253)

Destruction by plague:

> haec ratio quondam morborum et mortifer aestus
> finibus in Cecropis funestos reddidit agros
> vastavitque vias, exhausit civibus urbem.
> > (Lucr. 6.1138-1140)
> > nec singula morbi
> corpora corripiunt, sed tota aestiva repente
> spemque gregemque simul cunctamque ab origine gentem.
> > (*Geo.* 3.471-473)

sed si quem proles subito defecerit omnis
nec genus unde novae stirpis revocetur habebit.

                    (*Geo.* 4.281-282)

In each case the progression is the same, and in each the destruction is complete (this is as true for the bees as for the animals of the third book; *proles ... defecerit omnis* can hardly be more specific).[50] In fact, at least for Virgil, the pattern is even closer than indicated in the above examples. For in both instances, after relating the symptoms (3.440-444; 4.251-263), he recommends various treatments (3.445-469; 4.264-280), in whose spite calamity descends (3.471ff.; 4.281ff.).

And so, with characteristic irony, Virgil has undercut his suggestions about the immortality of the bees' society. Their race fails in spite of its social complexity and its high level of organization; ultimately the susceptibility which they share with the animal world is realized in precisely the same manner. This failure occurs, moreover, regardless of the indications which precede it (*non dubiis poteris cognoscere signis*, 4.253). With this statement we are firmly back in the tenuous world of the First Georgic, where the storm (1.311-334) and civil war (1.466-514) rendered ineffectual the signs which warned of their coming (*ut certis possemus discere signis*, 351; *sol tibi signa dabit*, 463). In the world of *labor* we have the ability to predict disaster, but that ability will not prevent its coming.

As with the livestock, where both the symptoms and results of the plague are seen in terms of extremes of temperature (3.441-444, 458-460, 479, 482-83, 500-501, 564-566), so with the bees, this phenomenon, which, as we have seen, operated as an active threat against their environment earlier in the book, also has a hand in their final calamity:

aut intus clausis cunctantur in aedibus omnes
ignavaeque fame et contracto frigore pigrae.

                    (4.258-259)

This aspect is stressed in a more allusive way through a group of Homeric similes (see Servius *ad* 4.261) which describe the sound made by the ailing bees:

frigidus ut quondam silvis immurmurat Auster,   (cold)
ut mare sollicitum stridit refluentibus undis,
aestuat ut clausis rapidus fornacibus ignis.   (heat)

                    (4.261-263)

Consider the original:

οὔτε θαλάσσης κῦμα τόσον βοάᾳ ποτὶ χέρσον,
παντόθεν ὀρνύμενον πνοιῇ Βορέω ἀλεγεινῇ.
οὔτε πυρὸς τόσσος γε ποτὶ βρόμος αἰθομένοιο
οὔρεος ἐν βήσσης, ὅτε τ᾽ ὤρετο καιέμεν ὕλην·
οὔτ᾽ ἄνεμος τόσσον γε περὶ δρυσὶν ὑψικόμοισι

ἠπύει, ὅς τε μάλιστα μέγα βρέμεται χαλεπαίνων,
κτλ.

(Il. 14.394-399)

The Homeric context, dealing as it does with the clash of battle, has no relevance for
Virgil; what attracted him was the presence of heat and cold. So he took over the
simile, compressed it, rearranged the Homeric order so as to make the similes for
heat and cold the frames, and defined Homer's bare ἄνεμος as frigidus Auster,
again in order to stress the effects of temperature.

Accepting the bees' society as approximate to that of man (and this is the point of
the ethnographical description), bound by the tenets of civilization and labor, we
can see in the loss of the bees the failure of that level of human society. In fact, this
view is foreshadowed by Virgil's implicating man in both plagues of the Georgics, at
the very close of the third book, and again in the fourth:

> verum etiam invisos si quis temptaret amictis,
> ardentes papulae atque immundus olentia sudor
> membra sequebatur, nec longo deinde moranti
> tempore contactos artus sacer ignis edebat.
>
> (3.563-566)
> si vero, quoniam casus apibus quoque nostros
> vita tulit, tristi languebunt corpora morbo –
> (4.251-252)

But what of the bugonia, "the resurrection of the bees ... the obvious answer to
the Plague of III".[51] Does this curious phenomenon redeem the despair which has
preceded it, and, for that matter, that which is to follow (as one critic has of late
pointedly remarked: "I cannot feel that the restoration of the bees outweighs the
suffering and death of Orpheus and Eurydice"[52])?

I would like first to look at the bugonia in a somewhat different way – namely in
its connection with the Italian, agricultural world. Seen from this viewpoint, it is no
solution at all. For the Georgics, to the extent that they define the realities of an
agricultural dilemma, end with the death of the hive, in mid-sentence, at 4.282.
What follows, bugonia and epyllion, is, of course, a part of the poem, but we should
not expect in these sections resolution of all the problems which have preceded.
Virgil, I believe, indicates his attitude towards this phenomenon, as clearly as he
possibly could, at the very outset of the account. He situates the bugonia:

> altius omnem
> expediam prima repetens ab origine famam.
> nam qua Pellaei gens fortunata Canopi
> accolit effuso stagnantem flumine Nilum
> et circum pictis vehitur sua rura phaselis,
> quaque pharetratae vicinia Persidis urget,

290

et diversa ruens septem discurrit in ora	292
usque coloratis amnis devexus ab Indis,	293
et viridem Aegyptum nigra fecundat harena,	291
omnis in hac certam regio iacit arte salutem.	294

(4.285-294)

A colourful ethnographical notice, whose tone will not have escaped Virgil's more knowledgeable reader; Virgil is preparing us for an Eastern *thaumasion*, pure and simple. If we believe it, that is, if we believe it has any application for the world of Italian civilization and agricultural activity, then we will believe in dragons' teeth and warrior harvests, in the other *thaumasia* which Virgil had previously distinguished in similar language, from the agricultural world as it really exists:

sed neque Medorum silvae, ditissima terra,
nec pulcher Ganges atque auro turbidus Hermus
laudibus Italiae certent, non Bactra neque Indi
totaque turiferis Panchaia pinguis harenis.
haec loca non tauri spirantes naribus ignem
invertere satis immanis dentibus hydri,
nec galeis densisque virum seges horruit hastis.

(2.136-143)

Nor does the *bugonia*, even if it were credible in an agricultural context, solve the problem of Aristaeus; for it in no way brings immortality, and a new hive produced by such means would be as susceptible as the old.[53]

As has recently been noted,[54] one of the main functions of the *bugonia* (and I believe it is *the* main function) is to provide a transition to the epyllion on Orpheus. In the *aetion* of this institution Virgil found the opportunity to produce his only neoteric epyllion, and one which he distinguished from previous instances by integrating it into a larger poetic context.

And what of this epyllion? Too much has been written on the matter, with any number of different conclusions,[55] and I shall confine myself to a brief examination of the figure of Orpheus, the central player in the episode, as it relates to the themes of this chapter and the last.

In the previous chapter it was suggested that Virgil presented in the *Georgics*, through the paradigms of the inhabitants of Italy and of Scythia, two cultural types which represent his attitude towards civilized agricultural endeavour: either man's *labor* is brought to nothing by the supremacy of post-Saturnian nature, or his success is qualified by the extent to which he must impose himself on and control the natural world. In opposition to these the old man of Tarentum was seen as the ideal – an individual explicitly excluded from the areas of modern agriculture, he attained a self-sufficiency through harmony with a nature which was both real (i.e. not artificially Saturnian) and cooperative.

As we have seen the first half of the Fourth Georgic, it stands as Virgil's implication of man (through the exemplum of the bees) in the downfall of his works (crops in Book 1, livestock in Book 3). In fact the entire fourth book can be seen as containing Virgil's judgement of the cultural levels with which the *Georgics* deal. In the *laudes Italiae* and at certain points through the second book, man's controlling force over nature was presented in negative terms. The second half of the fourth book, the epyllion on Orpheus, shows where the mentality motivated by such interests is led.

What is Orpheus for Virgil? David O. Ross has, in another context, most clearly defined the position of this figure for Virgil:[56]

"Orpheus has the power to charm nature, and, as it develops, the knowledge and understanding of it. The poetry Orpheus represents can thus properly be called scientific".

What I am suggesting is that Orpheus in the fourth book stands as a paradigm for the values exhibited in the technical sections of the poem by the modern Italian who has diverted nature to his will. As at the beginning of the second book the art of grafting resulted in the control and transformation of the natural world, and as throughout that book success is gained through a constant warfare on natural forces, so Orpheus had achieved a degree of control over nature:

> mulcentem tigris et agentem carmine quercus.
>
> (4.510)

Such control extended even to the Underworld:

> Taenarias etiam fauces, alta ostia Ditis,
> et caligantem nigra formidine lucum
> ingressus, Manisque adiit regemque tremendum
> nesciaque humanis precibus mansuescere corda.
>
> (4.467-470)

In this he is synonymous with the figure hailed at the end of the second book (*felix qui potuit rerum cognoscere causas/atque metus omnis et inexorabile fatum/subiecit pedibus strepitumque Acherontis avari*, 2.490-492).[57] But where does such control lead? In Orpheus' loss of Eurydice, it is rendered futile: *ibi omnis/effusus labor* (4.491-492). His labor is negated through personal loss.

Ultimately Orpheus learns the lesson. In the second book, the Italian *arator*, his agricultural counterpart, in moulding his environment, was compelled to commit an act against the natural world:

> aut unde iratus silvam devexit arator
> et nemora evertit multos ignava per annos,
> antiquasque domos avium cum stirpibus imis

eruit; illae altum nidis petiere relictis,
et rudis enituit impulso vomere campus.
                    (2.207-211)

In the end, in terms which can only be deliberate, Orpheus becomes the very object of this metaphor for man's moulding of nature, the *exemplum* for which he once stood:

qualis populea maerens philomela sub umbra
amissos queritur fetus, quos *durus arator*
observans nido implumis detraxit; at illa
flet noctem, ramoque sedens miserabile carmen
integrat, et maestis late loca quaestibus implet.
                    (4.511-515)

In his loss he becomes identical to the nightingale whose nest is pillaged by the ploughman. And so he ends, his failure complete, in a setting as hostile as that of the Scythian of the third book:

solus Hyperboreas[58] glacies Tanaimque nivalem
arvaque Riphaeis numquam viduata pruinis
lustrabat, raptam Eurydicen atque inrita Ditis
dona querens.
                    (4.517-520)

The susceptibility to failure of the ethics of *labor* is clearly demonstrable; nature's resurgence is evident in every aspect of existence. So in Books 1 and 3, and symbolically in his description of the bees' society Virgil demonstrated such shortcomings. Not so the shortcomings of the second level of cultural activity (the successful waging of war against nature – as it was presented in the *laudes Italiae* and the Second Georgic in general). The failure of this type is a spiritual failure, which Virgil could only suggest, not prove. Orpheus, then, is the *exemplum*, his fate the specific demonstration, if not the proof, that domination without consideration, control without empathy, must fail.

In the world after Saturn communal man has two choices, defeat at the hands of a resurgent nature, or resistance to, and domination of, those forces – temporarily successful, but eventually involving spiritual deprivation, and therefore ultimately flawed. There remains only the private world, the world of the Corycian, who understands nature's limitations, stays within them and thereby achieves individual success.

When Virgil began the closing paragraph of the *Georgics* with the words,

haec super arvorum cultu pecorumque canebam
et super arboribus,

he was not excluding the fourth book; rather he was referring explicitly to it.[59] For it is this book which elucidates the three preceding ones. In it are contained, on a higher poetic level, the major issues which concerned him in the "technical" parts of the poem, the issues which ultimately motivated this moving and curious masterpiece.

NOTES

1. For a convenient bibliographical survey on this matter (together with a perceptive study of the fourth book) see J. Griffin, "The Fourth *Georgic*, Virgil, and Rome", *GR* 26 (1979) 61-80.

2. The *topoi* identified by Dahlmann will be examined as they arise.

3. F. Klingner (*Virgils Georgica* [Zürich 1963] 243-244; *Virgil: Bucolica, Georgica, Aeneis* [Zürich 1967] 310-311, n. 1) first rejected Dahlmann's formal identification, although he agreed to some such influence. As E. W. Leach has recently noted, "Klingner's dismissal of this idea ... seems to have curtailed its further development by any scholar" ("*Sedes Apibus*: From the *Georgics* to the *Aeneid*", *Vergilius* 23 [1977] 15, n. 9).

4. This type is more literary in that it excludes material of a more detailed nature, and deals rather with generalities; see, e.g., Caesar, *B.G.* 5.13-14; Sallust, *B.J.* 17.3ff.; Mela 1.61, 3.25-32; Tac. *Agr.* 10-12.

5. E.g., Herod. 2.2-182 (Egypt), 4.5-82 (Scythia); Diod. 1.30ff. (Egypt), 3.1ff. (the Arabian Gulf); Strabo 15.1ff. (India). The most successful of this type is, of course, the *Germania*.

6. Cf. Dahlmann 550.

7. R. D. Williams, in a review of Dahlmann, *CQ* N.S. 6 (1956) 170.

8. *Virgils Georgica* (above, n. 3) 16.

9. Cf. Olck, "Biene", *RE* 3.466, for the reference to Cicero and Varro, *res rust.* 3.16.4.

10. While I do not suggest that Varro saw the bees in ethnographical terms, it is interesting that he used such diction, particularly when one considers his familiarity with the real tradition (on this, see above, Chapter II, n. 17).

11. It is the extensive nature of Virgil's approximation of the bees to men which is striking. Normally neither bees nor other creatures seem to constitute any exception to the Stoic separation of man from plants and animals (on the basis that man alone possesses *mens atque ratio* – precisely the characteristic of Virgil's bees). On this see Dahlmann 549. More generally, Cic., *fin.* 5.38-40; M. Pohlenz, *Die Stoa* I (Göttingen 1959) 56, 88-89; K. Reinhardt, "Poseidonios", *RE* 22.587-588. At best bees have only a *Gleich-als-ob* (ὡσανεί) *logos*, an attribute they share with a number of other animals; so Pohlenz I 40, 84, 147; II 49.

12. Dahlmann 551. We should, however, be somewhat wary of seeing such vocabulary as exclusively suggesting a human context. For many of the terms are also used by Virgil of other animals: *tectum* of cows and goats (*Geo.* 2.418, 3.317, 4.434), *statio* of gulls (*Aen.* 5.128), *cubile* of moles, birds and bulls (*Geo.* 1.183, 1.411, 3.230), *domus* of mice, birds, horses and goats (*Geo.* 1.182, 2.209, 3.96, *Ecl.* 4.21), *limen* of goats (*Geo.* 3.317) and *patria* of horses (*Geo.* 3.121). It is true, however, that the great concentration of such terminology in the description of the bees' society invites us to see such usage as more than merely "poetic" and to equate them with human society.

13. L. P. Wilkinson, *The Georgics of Virgil* (Cambridge 1969) 264.

14. L. Herrmann, "Le Quatrième Livre des Géorgiques et les Abeilles d'Actium", *REA* 33 (1931) 219-224; J. Perret, *Virgile, l'homme et l'oeuvre* (Paris 1952) 84; also Otis 181.

15. Above, n. 13, pp. 175-182.

16. Wilkinson sees in these lines a possible reminiscence of the sharing of quarters and communal attitude towards children as portrayed in Plato's *Republic* (connected, perhaps, with the mention of Athens at 4.177 – *Cecropias apes*). The context, however, seems to require a more general ethnographical parallel, for such detail is commonplace in the tradition: Herod. 1.216.1, 3.101.1, 4.172.2, 4.180.5; Ephorus *ap.* Strabo 7.3.7, 7.3.9; Caes. *B.G.* 5.14.4; 'Iambulus' *ap.* Diod. 2.58.1 (concerning the *beata insula* of the Indian Ocean); Lucian, *ver. hist.* 2.19. Generally, on this *topos*, cf. Schroeder 21ff.

17. So *lar* is used by Virgil not only for Trojans (*Aen.* 5.744) and Evander's community (*Aen.* 8.543) – instances which can be understood by extension – but also for Libyans (*Geo.* 3.344). *Penates* are given to both Greeks (*Aen.* 11.264) and Carthaginians (*Aen.* 4.21); such terms suggest the world of man, but need not imply a specifically Roman setting.

18. So Klingner, *Virgils Georgica* (above, n. 3) 244.

19. Dahlmann 561. For this objection, see Williams (above, n. 7) 170; Wilkinson (above, n. 13) 182, n.; Griffin (above, n. 1) 64.

20. For ethnographical references, see Schroeder 10ff.

21. So E. W. Leach (above, n. 3) 4.

22. Here see Schroeder's section, "Populi simplices matrimonium ignorantes feminas et liberos communes habent" (21).

23. Primitive societies are traditionally indolent: Herod. 2.116, 5.6.2; Tac. *Germ.* 14, 15; cf. Schroeder 16-18 for instances of this phenomenon ("otium amant, labores feminis mandant").

24. For the clearest exposition of the ethos of *labor* in Virgil, see Altevogt, *passim*. Those who would still see *labor* as a positive quality in the *Georgics* (e.g. Wilkinson [above, n. 13] 136, n.) must ignore the convincing evidence of this study.

25. The variants of this *aetion* are several. Hesiod (*Theog.* 453ff.) and Apollonius Rhod. (*Arg.* 2.1231-1241) have no mention of bees. Aratus (*Phaen.* 30-35) has the god nursed by bears. Callimachus (*Hymn* 1.49-50) merely states that honey first appeared on Mt. Ida while Zeus was being hidden there. Nicander

seems to have claimed that bees first came into existence in Crete in the time of Saturn (*sed ne illud quidem pertinet ad agricolas, quando et in qua regione primum natae sint* [*apes*] .. *an Cretae Saturni temporibus, ut Nicander,* Colum. 9.2.4). Euhemerus held that the bees were allotted honey in return for nursing the god (Colum. 9.2.3).

With such variety in the tradition Virgil was free to alter the *aetion* as he wished, which is, in fact, what he did. For him, honey existed before Jupiter's time – its spontaneous supply was a feature of the Saturnian age, and one which Jupiter on his ascendancy suppressed (*mellaque decussit foliis, Geo.* 1.131). Virgil's concern in the present lines was not with the birth of the bees nor the beginnings of honey, but rather with the genesis of the particular social institutions of their society (the lines immediately following the *aetion* effectively define *naturas*). It is these institutions, together with the emphasis on communal and unremitting *labor*, which compel us to see Jupiter's actions as a part of the transition from the age of Saturn. For differing views of these lines, cf. J. Lünenborg, *Das philosophische Weltbild in Vergils Georgika* (diss. Münster 1935) 23; Richter ad 4.149ff.; W. Frentz, *Mythologisches in Vergils Georgica,* Beitr. zur klass. Philol. 21 (1967) 60-68.

26. On the role of Jupiter in the *Georgics,* see Lünenborg (above, n. 25) 18-26.

27. Cf. 3.244, *amor omnibus idem.* Otis assumes (185) that because in this passage *amor* is viewed negatively, *labor omnibus unus* is to be seen as the positive antithesis to destructive *amor.* Rather both qualities are ultimately condemned; as Altevogt has shown, *labor* in the *Georgics* is a burden imposed on modern, agricultural man. In a broader context, Virgil seems to have seen a parallelism between these two forces and man's inability to free himself from their hold (*omnia vincit amor, Ecl.* 10.69; *labor omnia vicit/improbus, Geo.* 1.145-146); it is difficult to feel positively about either of these statements.

28. Here cf. the old man's late return (4.131-132), which is distinguished by his subsequent enjoyment of the fruits of his (individual) toil: *dapibus mensas onerabat inemptis.*

29. For the significance of *amor habendi* in this passage, see Altevogt 39-40. Also now M. C. J. Putnam, *Virgil's Poem of the Earth* (Princeton 1979) 258-259. Evander's speech will be examined in the next chapter.

30. The terms applied to the world of the bees (e.g. *fores, urbs, limina, domus, aula, regna, penates*) are features not of the rustic's tranquil landscape, but rather of the civilized man to whom he is opposed (2.461-466, 495-512; cf. *foribus domus alta superbis,* 461; *aulas et limina regum ... urbem miserosque penates,* 504-505). The *cerea regna* of the bees (4.202) perhaps remind us of the *res Romanae perituraque regna* of 2.498. Finally the warfare of the bees (*saepe duobus/regibus incessit ... discordia,* 4.68) again seems to indicate a parallel with this negative figure at the end of the second book (*infidos agitans discordia fratres,* 2.496).

31. In any case we should be on our guard with Virgil's statements about such immortality. In the main passage on this (4.219-227), the poet is pointedly detached: *his quidam signis ... dixere.* As E. M. Stehle has noted ("Virgil's *Georgics*: The Threat of Sloth", *TAPhA* 104 [1974] 360), this is probably a Stoic doctrine, which, as far as we can judge Virgil's philosophical outlook, should also lead us to reject such a view as being his own.

32. Klingner (*Virgils Georgica* [above, n. 3] 244) asserted with little argument that Dahlmann's identification of this category was fallacious; it should be clear from the instances of the *topos* which have so far been examined that the description of the bees' environment can legitimately be viewed as it was by Dahlmann.

33. Hipp. *aer.* 3-6; cf. also above, pp. 15-16, for this feature in Hor. *Epl.* 1.16.

34. Except for Columella, who cited the lines (9.4.1). Here and elsewhere Columella's obvious admiration for Virgil led him to accept and cite the poet on details which are not part of the technical tradition and which in some cases are probably Virgilian invention.

35. In this connection, see Richter 143-144, for parallels between Cato, Varro and *Geo.* 1.176ff. In line 181 of the passage given above there seems to be a reminiscence of *tum variae venere artes* (*Geo.* 1.145), perhaps the major feature of the coming of the age of Jupiter. The pernicious effects of mice, moles and the like provide a concrete example of the *labor improbus* connected with this age.

36. Here, then (unlike in the *laudes Italiae*), is the real Italian countryside.

37. For the close connection between this passage (3.414-439) and 4.242-247, see above, p. 82.

38. While Varro's observation is correct, the reason he attributes for the bees' actions (*ut bibere possint*) is mistaken; for the bees in fact collect droplets of water between their legs, return them to the hive, and by fanning with their wings ventilate the hive.

39. Richter (*ad loc.*) is incorrect in referring to Varro, *res rust.* 3.16.37 as a source; Varro was concerned with the effects of climatic extremes on the bees *outside* their hives, not in relation to the building of their entrances.

40. Columella's qualification may in fact be seen as a gentle correction of Virgil.

41. *Geo.* 1.335, 1.186, 2.333, 2.419, 4.37, 4.239; it is also noteworthy that *Metus* is personified and combined with *Morbi* at 3.552, with *Luctus, Curae, Egestas, Labos,* etc. in the Underworld at *Aen.* 6.276 (on this, see Altevogt 6-7, from the aspect of *Egestas* and *Labor*). B. Axelson (*Unpoetische Wörter* [Lund 1945] 127) has claimed that *timeo* is more common than *metuo* in "most" of the poets; this, however, seems to be the case only with Propertius and Tibullus (cf. *ThLL* 8.901-902).

42. There may be an additional connection in what appears to be a play between *fovere* (4.43) and *focis* (3.378). Varro's etymological explanation for *focus* is that it was so called because that is the place where fire is nurtured (*fovetur*, Varro ap. Serv. Auct. *ad Aen.* 11.211). Ovid was later to refer, in typical style, to this etymology: *at focus a flammis et quod fovet omnia dictus, Fast.* 6.301. There is support for the construct in Virgil in his continued emphasis on *fovere* (4.46, 56) and *focus* (4.48).

43. Note, too, in the same line *latebris* (*Geo.* 4.42) and *latebrae* (*Epist.* 1.16.15).

44. On this I admit despair; it may be that this curious detail is merely an example of a strong or unpleasant smell. It is perhaps interesting that it became part of the tradition (if, as seems likely, it was a Virgilian invention): Colum. 9.5.6; Plin. *N.H.* 11.62; cf. also Richter *ad* loc.; Gossen-Steier, "Krebs", *RE* 11.1669.

45. This parallel in diction is noted by Wilkinson (above, n. 13, 100).

46. The fact that Virgil will treat these lofty themes in this manner can be seen as a mitigation of the apparent reversal of poetic creed as stated in the Sixth Eclogue: *cum canerem reges et proelia, Cynthius aurem/ vellit et admonuit: 'pastorem, Tityre, pinguis/ pascere oportet ovis, deductum dicere carmen'* (3-5). On this see my note, "Ovid's Attempt at Tragedy (*Am.* 3.1.63-64)", *AJP* 99 (1978) 447-450.

47. Otis (177) says of these lines "The sheep are sensitive creatures who have to be protected against the *cold*: otherwise they will suffer, catch cold, *die*". Yet when he deals with the description of the bees' environment (which contains the same injunctions as appear in the third book), he can only conclude: "here man and nature are once more happily co-operating" (182).

48. The parallel seems clear, although critics have been unwilling to admit it; those who do, do so cautiously and avoid elaboration. So Richter (*ad* 4.251ff.): "eine Parallelität mit III möglich ist".

49. Again Otis of these lines from the third book: "Virgil prepares us for the finale (the overwhelming presence of death) by describing the dangers which ever beset the flocks" (179). While noting a general parallel in the fourth book (186-187), he minimizes it and moves quickly on to the account of Aristaeus (on which, see above, pp. 84-85).

50. Servius noted the progression of Virgil's account, as well as the emphatic tone of this final stage: *miro usus est ordine; nam primo ait quemadmodum animalia apibus inimica pellenda sint, deinde quibus medicaminibus morbo possint carere; nunc dicit penitus amissae qua possint ratione reparari* (*ad* 4.281).

51. Otis 188; so S. P. Bovie ("The Imagery of Ascent-Descent in Vergil's *Georgics*", *AJP* 77 [1956] 347), "Catastrophe reigns over the conclusion of the Third Book, elevation is restored at the end of the Fourth".

52. J. Griffin (above, n. 1) 71; Griffin is one of the few critics of Virgil prepared to doubt the generally accepted dictum that Book 4 (together with 2) is the "happy" counter to the "sad" Books 1 and 3.

53. At no point is Aristaeus given an antidote to the bees' *morbus*, although his mother claims he will receive one: *ut omnem/expediat morbi causam* (unless of course we accept the sin of Aristaeus as the cause, pure and simple – but such a realization will be of little value or comfort to the bee-keeper whose hive fails).

54. By M. C. J. Putnam (above, n. 29), 272.

55. J. Griffin (above, n. 1), 61-62, has a manageable summary of the 20-odd contributions to this question in the last two decades.

56. *Backgrounds to Augustan Poetry: Gallus, Elegy and Rome* (Cambridge 1975) 29; Ross is here concerned primarily with the figure of Orpheus as he represents a type of poetry (particularly in the Sixth Eclogue); however the cultural judgement holds true for Orpheus in a more general context. Cf. also Ross 94-95, 105, for Orpheus in the *Georgics*.

57. Again Ross (above, n. 56), 29-30, although in this also he treats the "poetic" rather than the "cultural" Orpheus.

58. This word appears only three times in all of Virgil's works; it is perhaps significant that it is used here to describe the setting of the defeated Orpheus, and at 3.381, in the account of the Scythian cave-dwellers.

59. *Haec ... canebam* can, of course, refer as easily to Book 4 as to the whole poem; in fact, it refers to both.

IV. CULTURAL POLEMICS IN THE *AENEID*

In recent years the *Aeneid* has evoked what can now be seen to be a coherent and progressive trend of criticism. Following an initial and necessarily somewhat extreme reaction against viewing the poem as representing Virgil's endorsement of the Augustan achievement (the *communis opinio*, it is fair to say, in Virgilian scholarship until the middle of this century),[1] there has emerged a more balanced attitude which can perhaps best be imparted by the following quotation, referring to the all but universal uneasiness which affects the reader as he reaches the end of the poem:[2]

> One may try to rationalize the dissatisfaction by proving the villainy of Turnus or by showing that the death of Turnus, the manner of his death, symbolizes the defeat of Juno; for those who are content to read the poem as an ethical melodrama, such solutions are apparently adequate – once we have separated the good guys from the bad guys and the bad guys get what is coming to them, the beauty of the poem is found to be intact. Thus, a solution we would find banal in any ephemeral movie of our choice is found to be adequate in the hands of an acknowledged master of Western epic. By the same token, it does no good to make Aeneas a monster, for that is to do no more than play the same game in a slightly more fashionable way: find the villain and call him an anti-hero. But in writing this poem, Vergil sought to imagine a world – or, rather, a complexity of worlds – that one or another kind of villain could not account for.

The practice of seeking villainy where it was not previously seen is a young one. If the following pages seem unduly directed towards such a practice, they should not be seen as representing a reading of the entire poem. Rather, as material contributing to the restoration of a more balanced attitude, from which the complexity of the poem may more fully emerge. That Virgil felt a degree of pride in his nation's achievement is undeniable, and it is not denied here. What I hope to suggest (as others have suggested) is that pride is in some ways qualified. At the same time, in that this is part of a broader study, we shall also see Virgil's attitudes in the *Aeneid* in relation both to his other poetry and to Roman poetry in general.

Let us begin with a positive cultural programme, the stated purpose of Augustus as prophesied by Anchises to Aeneas:

> hic vir, hic est, tibi quem promitti saepius audis,
> Augustus Caesar, divi genus, aurea condet
> saecula qui rursus Latio regnata per arva

Saturno quondam, super et Garamantas et Indos
proferet imperium.

(6.791-795)

The message is clear: Augustus is to establish in Latium a renewed golden age,
embracing under Roman rule the races of the world; in a word, *pax Augusta*, as
conceived by Augustus himself. The statement is unequivocal, the meaning on the
surface. It will be suggested in this chapter that beyond such open and accessible
dicta Virgil, in the second half of the poem, presented Aeneas and the Trojans (and
through them certain of the characteristics of the modern Roman[3]) in terms which,
from the viewpoint of theories of ethnography and cultural history, carry an
implicit criticism of the achievements of civilization. If so, the poet's technique is
parallel to that detected in the *Georgics*; the 'sinister' elements, in conflict with
wholly positive and blatant statement, exist on a more allusive and literary level, a
level at the same time of greater concealment.

But what is there of actual ethnography in the *Aeneid*? In terms of formal
instances of the tradition, there is nothing so elaborate or exact as the passages dealt
with in the *Georgics*. To some extent the poetic potential of ethnography had been
realized in this earlier work, and there is, of course, no reason why Virgil should
have repeated himself in his epic. There is in the *Aeneid* a great deal in the way of
descriptive epithets and phrases which, while they work largely on the level of
poetic embellishment, are at the same time residual features of the tradition with
which we are dealing (e.g. *vitrea ... Fucinus unda*, 7.759; *picti scuta Labici*, 7.796;
viridi gaudens Feronia luco, 7.800; *insula inexhaustis Chalybum generosa metallis*,
10.174).[4]

There are, however, two passages which contain 'significant' ethnographical
references, Evander's speech to Aeneas on the typology of Rome (8.314-336) and
the battle vaunt of Numanus Remulus (9.598-620).[5] Both are composed with great
care, and contain structural and thematic elements which suggest they are to be seen
as in some way complementary of each other.

Structure first: each extends over 23 lines and is preceded by a preamble of eight
lines (8.306-313; 9.590-597). The craft with which the actual speeches are written is
evident: in Evander's there is a movement from ethnographical material (five lines,
314-318) to mythical detail concerning the golden age (nine lines, 319-327), with
ethnographical elaboration (five lines, 328-332); finally, Evander relates his own
people's place in this cultural scheme (333-336). The speech of Remulus, as has been
noted,[6] is a perfect ring-composition: a pair of four lines open and close the passage
(598-601; 617-620); each is an invective-filled address to the Trojans. Immediately
within these is another pair, this time of three lines each (602-604; 614-616), setting
the basic contrast between Latin (*durum a stirpe genus*) and Trojan (*vobis ...
desidiae cordi*). And in the centre is an elaboration of the Italian way of life (605-
613). These nine lines are central in theme as well as structure, and it seems plausible

to suggest a deliberate parallel with the equally important nine lines at 8.319-327. This, however can only be a suggestion until the content of the two speeches is examined.

And it is content which binds the two passages. Each of them has a basis in the ethnographical traditions – indeed, they are the only passages in the poem to contain such material in any quantity. As will emerge, they are complementary pieces: the first (Evander to Aeneas) details the attitude of Evander's community to the Trojan arrival; the second (Numanus Remulus to Ascanius) that of the Latins – Troy, then, in relation to the entire Italian community. From both it may be possible to determine Virgil's view of the cultural changes which attend the infusion of the Trojan element into Italy.

The typology of Latium in the Eighth Aeneid has been repeatedly examined from the viewpoint of *Quellenforschung*. Many critics, on the basis of Seneca, *Epistle* 90, have proposed Posidonius as Virgil's source:[7] the role played by Saturn in Virgil's lines (319-327) is that of the *sapientes* who, in Seneca's summary of Posidonius, introduced the arts of civilization. From the evidence in Seneca's epistle, however, it is possible to assume that Posidonius is the source only for lines 319-325, and not for the whole passage; for, as far as we can tell, his account did not include a stage of primitive barbarism preceding the arrival and works of these *sapientes* (or at least it had no concern with such a stage). Posidonius may have provided Virgil with an impetus, in that he combined the concept of cultural progress with the Stoic golden age,[8] but for the Hellenistic philosopher this was all in the setting of the first stage of mankind (*primi mortalium*, Sen. *Epist.* 90.4). Virgil, on the other hand, postulated a prior stage (314-318), as well as a period of subsequent deterioration (326-332). Ultimately, then, the cultural theory of Posidonius, insofar as it can be reconstructed, cannot satisfactorily account for the entire sequence in Virgil's lines.

Others, on the basis of passages in Ennius (*Ann.* 25-28V, *Euhem., Var.* 64-97V) and Diodorus (5.66.4-6), have seen Euhemerus as Virgil's source.[9] Such a view is, on the face of it, unlikely, and in any case is open to the same objection – it does not account for the whole Virgilian sequence. In a more recent study[10] Callimachus is suggested (*Aet.* 3, fr. 75, 50-77). The parallels here, however, are rarely exact, as the author himself admits, and he seems unaware of the tradition of typology within ethnographical studies in general, a tradition which is crucial in identifying the sources from which Virgil drew (it may even be that Callimachus' source in this matter, Xenomedes of Ceos, was writing an ethnography of the island, ὅς ποτε πᾶσαν/νῆσον ἐνὶ μνήμῃ κάτθετο μυθολόγῳ, 54-55).[11]

H. Reynen, after summarizing the possible sources, and offering some useful remarks on Virgil's 'correction' of Lucretian anti-primitivism,[12] concluded:[13]

> Es ist gerade dies ein hohes Lob seiner Kunst, dass er das seiner Herkunft nach verschiedenartige Gedankengut so zu amalgamieren vermochte, dass man von der Voraussetzung einer einheitlichen Herkunft überhaupt ausgehen konnte. Er hat wirklich ein neues Ganzes geschaffen.

This is, of course, precisely what we expect of Virgil, traditional elements put to a new and original use. And yet, the nature of these traditional elements will be important in divining Virgil's ultimate intent, and, I believe, in this, there are still certain observations to be made.

What appears at *Aen.* 8.314-336 is a merging of two traditions of cultural history, the one loosely 'scientific', the other of a more mythical nature, whose divisions are strictly reflected in the compositional breakdown of the passage (above, p. 94): under the 'scientific' heading belong the two groups of five lines each (314-318, 328-332). If these lines are taken as a single whole they exactly resemble descriptions of *gentes* as they appear in ethnographical studies. Indeed there seems to be a conscious reminiscence of Sallust's Libyan ethnography, a passage which will doubtless have been accessible to Virgil. The similarities can best be shown by the following:[14]

Sall. *B.J.* 18.1-19.2	Virg. *Aen.* 8.314-318, 328-332
Africam initio habuere Gaetuli et Libyes	haec nemora indigenae Fauni Nymphaeque tenebant[15]
asperi incultique	quis neque mos neque cultus[16] erat
quis cibus erat caro ferina atque humi pabulum uti pecora	sed rami atque asper victu venatus alebat
ii neque moribus neque lege aut imperio quoiusquam regebantur	(neque mos neque cultus)
vagi palantes quas nox coegerat sedes habebant	nec iungere tauros/ aut componere opes norant aut parcere prato
Medi, Persae et Armenii in Africam transvecti ... locos occupavere, et.	tum manus Ausonia et gentes venere Sicanae

As is clear from this, the movement is the same in both accounts: both begin with the aboriginal inhabitants, describing their salient characteristics (in each case the emphasis is on the absence of the arts of civilization, and the wording is parallel at a number of points), and ending with a survey of the various waves of migration.[17]

Into this traditional ethnographical material, Virgil inserted the mythical account of Saturn's exile and flight to Latium, together with the subsequent degeneration (319-327). The final four lines (333-336) place Evander and his people in this scheme; they are the last group to settle before the arrival of the Trojans.

This, then, is the fabric of Evander's speech. Virgil, in effect, has intermeshed two separable descriptions of cultural change, producing an untraditional, seemingly original scheme. The result is to some extent a conflicting one. On the one hand there is, in the central panel (319-327), traditional primitivism: the blessings of the Saturnian age degenerate into a *decolor aetas*, characterized by warfare and rapacity. On the other, by positing a ruder, uncivilized state before Saturn's rule, Virgil has created of Saturn a culture-hero, who appears much like the Posidonian *sapientes*. And finally, further decline (328-332), associated with hostile migrations to Latium. If the separate components of the speech are recognized, it becomes clear that there is no single, specific source for Virgil's depiction of Latium's cultural history;[18] he has instead presented a unique and individual account.

The next, and the obvious, question is 'What is the significance of this typology in the *Aeneid?*' It has been supposed by some that it is intended to establish a series of cultural stages, occurring before the arrival of the Trojans, and serving as a framework for future change down to the Rome of Augustus; specifically to support Anchises' prophecy to Aeneas in the sixth book:[19]

> hic vir, hic est tibi quem promitti saepius audis,
> Augustus Caesar, divi genus, aurea condet
> saecula qui rursus Latio regnata per arva
> Saturno quondam.
>
> (6.791-794)

As Saturn once did, so also Aeneas,[20] and through him Augustus, will restore the golden age to Latium. And yet, in spite of Anchises' prophecy, such an outcome is never specified in the poem; indeed, it appears to be deliberately avoided. If we leave aside this prophecy (presented on the level of blatant statement), if we examine the action in the 'Italian' second half of the *Aeneid*, in other words, if we extend Evander's typology from the point at which it breaks off through the remainder of the poem, a very different picture emerges. The addition of the Trojan element, as it appears in the *Aeneid* at any rate, is to be seen as continuing the decline that follows Saturn: *et belli rabies et amor successit habendi* (8.327); what line would better describe *Aeneid* 7-12? Do the waves of Ausonian and Sicanian migrations have any greater effect in speeding the end of the Saturnian land than do the Trojans? Not in this poem certainly.

But the *pax Augusta* is promised. Surely then, we expect some mention of it, and we expect it at the end of this same book, in the description of Aeneas' shield. We expect the fulfilment of Anchises' injunction:

> tu regere imperio populos, Romane, memento,
> hae tibi erunt artes, pacique imponere morem,
> parcere subiectis et debellare superbos.
>
> (6.851-853)

But there is no such fulfilment; as one critic has noted: "Virgil's failure to speak of the Augustan age as the ultimate completion of the historical process has been noted but brushed aside".[21] Half of the prophecy has been fulfilled, as the description of the shield closes with the world subjected (*incedunt victae longo ordine gentes*, 722), a subjection in which the natural world is unwillingly implicated (*et pontem indignatus Araxes*, 728 – the last item on the shield).[22] If the *Aeneid* expresses a failure of any sort, it is that it does not get beyond this point.

And what of the speech of Numanus Remulus, expressing as it does the Latin attitude to the Trojan infusion? Its details have been well documented, their dependence on the ethnographical tradition established.[23] There is no need here to repeat the list of Virgil's sources. The picture of the early Latins is a composite of characteristics conventionally ascribed by ethnographers to primitive, uncivilized societies. Their *duritia*, their dependence on hunting, their *patientia* (agricultural as well as military),[24] the continuance of their strength into old age, and their subsistence on plunder are all features ascribed by civilized Greek and Roman authors to uncivilized peoples.[25] Inextricably tied to such features, moreover, is the implication of a high moral excellence, usually in contrast to the weaknesses of the writer's own advanced society; in short, "The vigor, courage, endurance of body and spirit are linked with the hardy conditions of the simple life and its satisfactions".[26]

How, then, are we to see these lines, and how the clear contrast between them and the framing verses on the weakness and effeminacy of the Trojans (598-602, 614-620)? Again, the details of the description of the Trojans and their traditional nature have been well covered.[27] The picture is one of total degeneracy, and, in ethnographical terms, these "Phrygians" are assigned all the attributes of a society which, in its advance along the scale of civilization, has become completely corrupt. From the passage taken as a whole, and from the contrast it sets up, at least by the standards of ancient thinking on morality, it seems necessary to recognize in Numanus' speech a condemnation of the debilitating qualities which the Trojans are in the process of importing to Italy, which is to recognize the Latins as the defenders of a morally desirable (if doomed) cultural heritage. Virgil here, as elsewhere, recognized that the age of Jupiter was a necessity, but that does not imply approval.

This apparently necessary conclusion is absent even from the works of those critics who have rightly identified the sources from which Virgil drew. It will perhaps be worthwhile to summarize in brief the various critical views. H. J. Schweizer, in focusing only on the central line of Numanus' speech (*omne aevum ferro teritur*, 609), and interpreting it as evidence that the Latins represent an iron age society (to be replaced by Aeneas' [Augustus'] renewal of the golden age), was compelled to ignore the remainder of the speech – the characterization of the Trojans as effeminate and morally corrupt is hardly compatible with any description of the world under Saturn.[28] And, as pointed out, in ethnographical terms, the culture of the Latins is to be seen as a positive, not a negative, one. N. Horsfall, whose study of this passage is both thorough and perceptive, nevertheless concludes with a largely unqualified view of its indicating the attainment of a positive *pax Augusta*.[29] M. E. Taylor, who also identified the cultural theory behind the passage, proceeded to introduce the *violentia* of Numanus,[30] and suggest that Virgil, having presented the description of the Latins in primitivist terms, then adopted an anti-primitivist stance (such as occurs nowhere else in his poetry), thereby justifying the nature of the Trojan culture.[31] This seems somewhat at variance with her claim, made earlier, that at the centre of the speech "we have the values of the hard primitivist and the poet's evident endorsement of the spirit".[32] One critic[33] has even suggested that the word *desidiae*, applied to the Trojan way of life (615), may be a veiled compliment, referring to the "sophisticated abandonment of the typical Roman way of life"; this is clearly impossible in this context.[34] Another[35] discounts this depiction of the Trojans (together with others which impugn their cultural background) on the grounds that such charges are only made by the enemies of Aeneas. We would hardly expect an admission on the part of the Trojans themselves. The speech of Numanus Remulus may be an example of rhetorical *vituperatio*,[36] but to identify it as such is not to explain its function in the poem; the careful contrast which Virgil builds in these lines suggests that they represent more than a battle vaunt, to be rejected as the rhetoric of an enemy.

I have given this survey because it exposes a common approach to *Aen.* 9.598-620. Each of the critics who have dealt with the lines seems to overcome an apparent uneasiness about them by rationalizing elements of the speech, which, without that rationalization, might compel us to ascribe to Virgil a not altogether positive attitude towards the Trojans' coming to Italy. We have already seen (above, pp. 38-50) that Virgil, in the *laudes Italiae*, suggested that Rome's greatness was tempered by those moral flaws which attend societies at an advanced point of civilization.[37] The speech of Numanus is relevant to this theme: the decay in Virgil's Rome can be seen to have its seeds in the effeminacy, *luxuria* and lack of moral hardiness which is imputed as a part of the Trojan character. There is here, I think, somewhat more than "a trace of hesitation and hostility towards the Trojans";[38] rather, at the very genesis of the Roman state, there is a flawed element which will be transmitted to the present, and realized in the moral degeneracy which is a part (and only a part) of modern Roman civilization.[39]

In this connection, it is worth mentioning the prayer of Iarbas to Jupiter in the fourth book; his charges against the Trojans are virtually identical to those of Numanus:

> et nunc ille Paris cum semiviro comitatu,
> Maeonia mentum mitra crinemque madentem
> subnexus, rapto potitur.
>
> (4.215-217)[40]

It may be no accident that this prayer (4.206-218) and the speech of Numanus appear in balancing positions in terms of the whole poem – 200 lines into the fourth book, and 200 lines from the end of the ninth. Again, if we wish, we may see this as merely the rhetoric of a hostile figure, to be recognized as such and therefore discredited. Or it may be another indication that the Trojan element, one of the main components of the Roman state, possesses negative moral characteristics which will manifest themselves in Virgil's contemporary society.

The purpose of this study has been to suggest that Virgil's attitude to his contemporary world, as expressed through ethnographical material in the *Aeneid*, was at least ambivalent, that there are prices which a society, in the process of becoming culturally 'successful', must pay. As in the *Georgics*, so here, the ambivalence rests on two phenomena. In attaining civilization man must exert force and destroy; Evander's community must be disrupted, Pallas, the last hope of an aging king,[41] must die, as the retreat from the golden age becomes complete. At the same time the desirable but impracticable simplicity and primitive hardiness of man in his primal state must be replaced by a degeneracy which (in terms of Roman thought) inevitably attends the civilizing process. For Rome to become Rome, both must happen; that, however, need not imply that the observer of the process (no matter how great his pride in the achievement) will wholeheartedly and without reservation applaud.[42]

Departing now from the poem's ethnographical material, I would like to examine the way in which, in the seventh book of the *Aeneid*, from the point of their arrival in Italy, the Trojans are presented as the element which motivates the change from the age of Saturn to that of Jupiter – a necessary cultural development, but one which in Roman poetry is consistently attended with a note of regret.[43] If this is in part Virgil's theme in the second half of the *Aeneid*, then it will again be plausible to suggest that he has allusively undercut his more open claim that the golden age is in the process of being restored to Latium.

At the beginning of the seventh book (37-45), Virgil, more personally visible than at any other point in the poem, announces his new theme; he will tell of the Trojans' reaching their goal, of the outbreak of war and all Hesperia under arms. The tone at this point is particularly elevated:

> maior rerum mihi nascitur ordo,
> maius opus moveo.
>
> (44-45)

The phrase *nascitur ordo* appears only once elsewhere in the works of Virgil; the sense is somewhat different, but the recall seems deliberate:

> magnus ab integro saeculorum nascitur ordo.
> (*Ecl.* 4.5)

Here of course the theme is the rolling back of the ages, and on the surface at least it may be that Virgil intended us to notice the similarity, to be expecting the theme of cultural transition. The very next words appear to support such a view:

13. Above, n. 7, 425.

14. Rehm (above, n. 4) 64, n. 139, merely cites this reference, together with Thucydides 6.2.2; Dion. Hal. *Ant. Rom.* 1.9ff.; Pliny, *N.H.* 3.56; Tac. *Germ.* 2-4. The proximity between Sallust's and Virgil's accounts warrants closer examination, particularly since his footnote has escaped the notice of subsequent critics. The *Histories* of Sallust also offer a tantalizing reference which at least allows us to speculate that it may have been a source for Virgil; Sallust is writing an ethnography of the region around the Taurus: *genus hominum vagum et rapinis suetum magis quam agrorum cultibus, Hist.* 2, fr. 85 M. (cf. *Aen.* 8. 315-318).

15. The verbs *habere* and *tenere* are regularly used at the outset not only of such accounts as these, but also of historical works in general; a few examples will suffice: Lucr. 4.580; Sall. *B.C.* 6.1; Livy 1.1.3, 1.1.5; Tac. *Ann.* 1.1.1.

16. Significantly, Servius Auctus comments: *NEQUE CULTUS ERAT: alii ad animum referunt, ut Sallustius indocti incultique* (*ad Aen.* 8.316). The reference is to *B.C.* 2.8; yet the parallel from the ethnography of Libya seems even closer (particularly when one looks to *Aen.* 8.316, *asper ... venatus*).

17. It should not go unnoticed in this connection that Hercules, although not mentioned in Evander's actual typology, plays an important role in the cultural development as it appears in the eighth book, and also has a part in the migrations in Sallust's account. For the central position of Hercules throughout ethnographical studies, see Norden, *Die germanische Urgeschichte* 171-182.

18. Generally, on the blending of separate theories of cultural development, see Burton (above, n. 8) 47ff.; also L. Koenen, "Papyrology in the Federal Republic of Germany and Fieldwork of the International Photographic Archive in Cairo", *Studia Papyrologica* 15 (1976) 53-54.

19. Binder (above, n. 3) has investigated the question of parallel characterization in the Eighth Aeneid (80-111). Few would object to some of his views; e.g. that Aeneas and Augustus are in some ways parallel. With other combinations, however (e.g. Hercules-Aeneas-Augustus/Cacus-Turnus-Antony, 141-149), he risks creating of the *Aeneid* a mere historical allegory.

20. So H. J. Schweizer (above, n. 6) 18. As Saturn tamed and brought laws to the *indigenae* of Italy, so Aeneas is in the process of taming and civilizing the Latins. Such a view, although neat, must overlook the essential discrepancy between the activities of the two; Saturn operates specifically outside the sphere of military action, which can hardly be said for Aeneas, at least not for the Aeneas of the *Aeneid*.

21. D. S. Wiesen, "The Pessimism of the Eighth Aeneid", *Latomus* 32 (1973) 756; at a number of points this article offers some perceptive comments on Virgil's ambivalence.

22. On this see above, chapter 2, pp. 43-4. For those who claim that a shield deals properly only with militaristic themes, reference need only be given to *Il.* 18.607-608 (the closing lines of Homer's description), where a river is also included, but in a very different manner: ἐν δὲ τίθει ποταμοῖο μέγα σθένος Ὠκεανοῖο/ἄντυγα πὰρ πυμάτην σάκεος πύκα ποιητοῖο.

23. B. Rehm (above, n. 4) 67-68; Schweizer (above, n. 6) 14-20; most extensively, N. Horsfall, "Numanus Remulus: Ethnography and Propaganda in *Aen.*, ix, 598f.," *Latomus* 30 (1971) 1108-1116; also very useful, although it has escaped the notice of most critics of these lines, is M. E. Taylor, "Primitivism in Virgil", *AJP* 76 (1955) 270-272.

24. As Horsfall has noted (above, n. 23), 1111, this particular feature sets these early Latins in the same sphere as the idealized rustic at the end of *Georgics* 2 (cf. above, pp. 46-7), although the intensity of the *patientia* is greater in Numanus' speech, and it also lacks any golden age idealization. The positive side of this quality, however, is still quite apparent.

25. On this, see Schroeder 15-16, 44; for the specific sources of Virgil's lines, Horsfall (above, n. 23) 1109-1113.

26. So Taylor (above, n. 23) 271.

27. Mainly by Horsfall (above, n. 23) 1113-1115.

28. Schweizer (above, n. 6) 16-20; as Horsfall has pointed out (above, n. 23), 1110, this reference must remain uncertain from the standpoint of any fixed theory of Kulturgeschichte.

29. Although he states "Virgil seems to retain a trace of hesitation and hostility towards the Trojans" (1116), to resolve the ambivalence expressed in this passage, Horsfall must return to the injunction of Anchises to Aeneas (*memento ... debellare superbos*, 6.851-853), a prophecy which, as we have suggested, is never realized in its *full* sense in *Aeneid* 7-12.

30. This rationale is much like that used by critics to overcome uneasiness at the death (or manner of death) of Turnus.

31. Taylor (above, n. 23) 272-273.

32. Ib. 271.

33. K. Quinn, *Virgil's Aeneid, A Critical Description* (London 1968) 209.

34. In the present context, *desidiae cordi* can only be pejorative (cf. Cic. *Verr.* 2.7, 2.76; Sall. *B.C.* 2.5, 53.5; Tac. *Hist.* 3.47; also see Horsfall [above, n. 23] 1114). In any case, even in the five instances of the word from Roman elegy (Prop. 1.12.1, 1.15.6; Ovid, *Am.* 1.9.31, *R.A.* 149, *Trist.* 3.7.31), the word hardly has a positive force; at best it is equivalent to the destructive *otium* of Catullus 51. Essentially it does not seem to lose its purely pejorative force before Statius, for whom it can have the neutral sense of *quies* (cf. *ThLL* 5.711.84ff.).

35. W. Suerbaum, "Aeneas zwischen Troja und Rom; Zur Funktion der Genealogie und der Ethnographie in Vergils *Aeneis*", *Poetica* 1 (1967) 200.

36. R. Heinze (above, n. 6) 422-423, and G. Highet (*The Speeches of Vergil's Aeneid* [Princeton 1972] 89-90, 257-258) also deal with the speech in terms of its dependence upon rhetorical theory.

37. Above, chapter 2, pp. 38-50.

38. Horsfall (above, n. 23) 1116.

39. When a Roman author deals with moral decline in terms such as appear from Numanus' speech, it is difficult to avoid seeing a contemporary reference.

40. Heinze (above, n. 6), 269, has remarked that this speech and that of Numanus Remulus have a common theme.

41. In Roman poetry the premature death of a sole child is attended by an unequalled sense of pathos and loss; cf. Cat. 64.215-237 (lines which may well have been in Virgil's mind at *Aen.* 8.574-584); so *Aen.* 9.473-497 (Euryalus' mother); also, for that matter, the dialogue of Priam and Achilles in *Iliad* 24.

42. Nor that he will necessarily condemn the society resting on such foundations; merely that he will realize its defects.

43. This is as true for Virgil as it is for Horace, Tibullus and (perhaps) Ovid.

44. On this, see Conington, *ad loc.*; Binder (above, n. 3) 96-97.

45. The first alternative, which Virgil clearly intends at 8.322, is a derivation from *latere* (because Saturn hid there – *latuit*); see Enn. *Euhem. Var.* 97 V; Serv. *ad Aen.* 8.322; also Binder (above, n. 3) 85, n. 42. The other explanation is that Latinus was king there – hence Latium; cf. Varro, *ling lat.* 5.32; Serv. Auct. *ad Aen.* 8.322, *quidam ferunt a Latino dictum Latium* (*alii ipsum Latinum a Latio*).

46. E.g., V. Buchheit, *Vergil über die Sendung Roms*, Gymnasium Beihefte 3 (1963) 93; also Reynen (above, n. 7) 423; Binder (above, n. 3) 97.

47. On this, see Binder (above, n. 3) 90; in a different context, Schroeder 41-44; Reynen (above, n. 7) 423.

48. Such triple anaphora of a common name is extremely rare in Virgil, and is clearly intended as very emphatic; cf. *Ecl.* 3.60-61, where the names are, however, repeated only once: *Iove ... Iovis; Phoebus ... Phoebo.*

49. On this, see particularly J. K. Newman (above, n. 1) 262-264 – in effect a review of Otis' interpretation of the end of the *Aeneid.*

50. Otis 377; I can find no indication (indeed the reverse seems to hold) before Allecto's visitation and her infliction of *furor* on Turnus to support such a view. This even appears in his gentle (if foolish in the circumstances) admonishing of the demonic deity.

51. Johnson (above, n. 2) 137; in fact, these lines were directed against Tiberius (p. 122 Morel), but they can, I think, be seen as a general commentary on the principate.

V. THE STOIC LANDSCAPE OF LUCAN 9

In coming to Lucan we leave behind the immediate development which has been traced so far. And yet, as is by now clear, the tradition of ethnographical writing is a continuous one; accordingly it remains accessible to the poet regardless of his age. That Lucan was generally aware of, and that he to some degree drew from, this tradition has been realized, and, indeed, a certain number of studies have dealt with the subject. There have been general works on his approach to geography and ethnography in the *Pharsalia*,[1] and even studies of specific geographical areas.[2] However, it is fair to note that each of these is predominantly concerned either with recovering the sources of Lucan in this matter, or with speculation on the extent to which the poet's actual information can be verified.[3] Poetic function is rarely considered.

This gives rise to a broader problem; speaking in a different context, Lucan's greatest critic noted: "The art of understanding Lucan makes no steady and continuous progress, and relapse accompanies advance". The critic of Lucan's artistry is faced with a special problem. When approaching Augustan poetry, we feel at ease in seeing significance in verbal reminiscence, in a particular stylistic or metrical feature, even in the use of a particular word. The stated creed was one of attention to detail and the poetry is to be read accordingly. Not so with Lucan. Partly because of his own youth (and the relative haste with which his epic must have been composed), partly because of the apparently artificial nature of his language, and perhaps most importantly because unlike the neoteric or Augustan poet he appears to belong to no identifiable literary movement, critical assessment of the *Pharsalia* is by no means an easy task. While it is not intended in this chapter to assert or deny Lucan's general artistic abilities, by examining his poetic application of the ethnographical tradition, we may demonstrate that in one area at least his poetry is neither haphazard nor without a high degree of consciousness of the possibilities contained in traditional literary material.

The only complete ethnographical description in the *Pharsalia* is that of Libya in the ninth book (411-444). It has never actually been identified as such,[4] and treatment of it has, on the whole, been confined to *Quellenforschung* on details of the account.[5] Studies specifically on Book 9, treating it as a "digression", virtually ignore it.[6] Morford in particular seems to view the passage chiefly as evidence for the poet's training in rhetoric.[7] Our purpose here is to examine the description in the light of the tradition to which it belongs, and from there to observe the ways in which it may contribute to Lucan's poetic intentions in the poem – specifically to his depiction of the character of Cato.[8]

The description of Libya, then, although somewhat abbreviated, is complete as an ethnography. Lucan began, as he was virtually required to do, with a statement on the land's *situs* (411-420), first in relation to the rest of the known world:

> tertia pars rerum Libye, si credere famae
> cuncta velis; at, si ventos caelumque sequaris,
> pars erit Europae.
>
> (411-413)

From the outset, Lucan has demonstrated his familiarity with the tradition, for these lines reflect precisely the debate over the position of Africa: is it a third continent (as most believe), or merely a part of Europe, with the Straits of Gibraltar serving as a hinge between the two?[9] Also significant in establishing his familiarity with the genre is Lucan's use of the parenthesis, *si credere famae/cuncta velis* (411-412); as was shown above,[10] such expressions occur frequently in ethnographical descriptions, be they normal or fantastic in nature. Lucan concludes this category with theoretical arguments, based on measurements and winds (413-420); this is reminiscent above all of Strabo's treatment of the lands of the world.[11]

From this point the account takes on a tone which is relevant to Lucan's larger purpose in the ninth book. In describing each of the features of Libya, he stresses the harshness of the environment and the resulting hardiness and primitiveness of its inhabitants. While it is certainly the case that this area is not one of the world's most pleasant, Lucan, as we shall see, deliberately suppresses elements (which exist in the prose tradition) which would detract from his depiction of the land as a bleak and hostile setting.

First climate:

> temperies vitalis abest, et nulla sub illa
> cura Iovis terra est; natura deside torpet
> orbis et immotis annum non sentit harenis.
>
> (435-437)

For the hexameter, Lucan employs Horace's *temperies* (above, p. 11), although here, of course, the opposite situation pertains: such balance is absent,[12] to the point that life itself (*vitalis*) cannot be supported. The land is literally god-forsaken, there are no seasons, no ploughing.[13] This last deficiency, the absence of ploughing, is, throughout ethnographical accounts, an indication of primitiveness.[14]

This treatment of climate stands in the midst of the category dealing with agricultural produce and mineral wealth (420-434; 438-440). Here Lucan was quick to dismiss the positive side:

> Libycae quod fertile terraest
> vergit in occasus; sed et haec non fontibus ullis
> solvitur.
>
> (420-422)

Even to this point, Sallust's account was not so bleak; indeed, for him, as in fact, of the three agricultural pursuits, two flourished in Libya: *ager frugum fertilis, bonus pecori, arbori infecundus* (*B.J.* 17.5). Lucan, moreover, focused mainly on the barren areas around the Syrtes, thereby giving an overall impression of agricultural desolation:

> at, quaecumque vagam Syrtim complectitur ora
> sub nimio proiecta die, vicina perusti
> aetheris, exurit messes et pulvere Bacchum
> enecat et nulla putris radice tenetur.
> (431-434)

Again the familiar tricolon: no crops, no vines, no pasture.[15] Three lines later (after treatment of climate) the category is resumed, as Lucan relates the actual produce:

> hoc tam segne solum raras tamen exerit herbas,
> quas Nasamon, gens dura, legit, qui proxima ponto
> nudus rura tenet.
> (438-440)

In spite of their being excluded from conventional agricultural pursuits, the hardy inhabitants (*gens dura*) manage to eke out subsistence from a hostile environment. Now what we have here is precisely the same movement, and in part the same diction, as that employed by Virgil in his tricolon dealing with the agricultural activities of the old man of Tarentum:[16]

> cui pauca relicti
> iugera ruris erant, nec fertilis illa iuvencis
> nec pecori opportuna seges nec commoda Baccho.
> *hic rarum tamen* in dumis olus albaque circum
> lilia verbenasque premens ...
> (*Geo.* 4.127-131)

Both passages are poetic ethnographies, and in both negation of the three standard areas of civilized agriculture is followed by some form of redemption.

In chapter 2 we argued that the Corycian's environment was successful in terms which deliberately excluded civilized agriculture. We shall see that Lucan's intent is somewhat different, but that he, like Virgil, was concerned to express approval for a society which survived outside of the tenets of civilization.[17]

Mineral resources constitute a subdivision of this category, and in Lucan's account they receive rather disproportionate elaboration:

> in nullas vitiatur opes; non aere nec auro
> excoquitur, nullo glaebarum crimine pura
> et penitus terra est. tantum Maurusia genti

barbarian Scythian. Specifically the barbarian has no use for gold and silver, or for wealth in general, he eats, dwells and dresses with the utmost simplicity, and lives in a society where *iustitia* is upheld without the necessity of laws. Not only does philosophy endorse such societies; it also states that in spite of its own efforts it is inferior (*quod Graeci longa sapientium doctrina praeceptisque philosophorum consequi nequeunt*).

In the second book of the *Pharsalia*, then, Cato is carefully described in terms which elsewhere in Stoic world-philosophy were applied to the primitive inhabitants of foreign lands, as they were ideally envisaged. It is this approximation that we must take with us to the ninth book, when Cato next appears, the sole survivor of Republican *virtus*. It is, moreover, in this light that we must view his relationship to the Libyan ethnography of that book.

By now the qualities of *duritia* and *patientia*, as assigned to primitive races, are quite familiar.[33] Sallust's Africans (*patiens laborum, B.J.* 17.6) and Lucan's Nasamones (*gens dura*, 9.439) are just two examples. Now this terminology also appears to have been a part of the currency of Stoicism:

> nulla itaque res magis iracundiam alit quam luxuria intemperans et impatiens: dure tractandus animus est ut ictum non sentiat nisi gravem.
> (Sen. *de ira* 2.25.4)[34]

Spiritual hardiness must prevail over *luxuria*, a commonplace enough idea. And yet Seneca was also clearly familiar with such terminology in its ethnographical context:

> quid enim est aliud quod barbaros tanto robustioribus corporibus, tanto patientiores laborum comminuit nisi ira infestissima sua?
> (*de ira* 1.11.1)

Lucan in the ninth book applied this vocabulary to the figure of Cato in a highly conscious manner; in this he can only have intended to extol him both as a Stoic hero and, more importantly, as a character at harmony with the harsh environment in which he is set. In that Cato's *patientia* and even the march itself do not occupy an unduly large place in the biographical tradition,[35] we can assume that this emphasis is Lucan's own contribution.

At the end of Cato's speech in which he warns his troops of the hazards of Libya (379-406), and just a few lines before the ethnography of that land, Lucan stressed the concept:

> serpens, sitis, ardor harenae
> dulcia *virtuti*; gaudet *patientia duris*.
> (402-403)

And again, immediately following the description of Libya, and five lines after reference to its hardy inhabitants, the Nasamones (*gens dura*):

                                  hac ire Catonem
dura iubet *virtus.*

                                      (444-445)

It is within this context, between Cato's exhortation for *patientia* and his actual
embarking on the ordeal, that the ethnography is set; far from being a 'digression',
this description is central to an understanding of the light in which Lucan has
presented Cato in the ninth book. Cato himself, after the first of the desert
hardships, the sandstorm, confirms his *patientia* when it had been impugned by a
soldier's offering him a helmetful of water:

    usque adeo mollis[36] primisque caloribus impar
    sum visus?

                                      (507-508)

   In fact, throughout the book, Lucan artfully varied the concepts with which we
have been dealing, constantly stressing Cato's *patientia* and *duritia*, and the ways in
which he instilled these qualities in his men:

    ast illae puppes luctus planctusque ferebant
    et mala vel *duri* lacrimas motura Catonis.
                                      (49-50)

                          sic voce Catonis
    inculcata viris iusti *patientia* Martis.
                                      (292-293)

    durum iter ad leges patriaeque ruentis amorem.
                                       (385)

    hi mihi sint comites, quos ipsa pericula ducent
    qui me teste *pati* vel quae tristissima pulchrum
    Romanumque putant.
                                      (390-392)

                      durae saltem *virtutis* amator
    quaere quid est virtus et posce exemplar honesti.
                                      (562--563)

    has inter pestes *duro* Cato limite[37] siccum
    emetitur iter.
                                      (734-735)

               sic *dura* suos *patientia* questus
    exonerat. cogit tantos *tolerare labores*
    summa ducis *virtus.*
                                      (880-882)

   In addition, the poet plays on the possible meanings of *patientia*, in both Stoic and ethnographical senses. At the beginning of the book, Pompey's soul, before settling in Cato's body, joins the lower aether:

> semidei manes habitant, quos *ignea virtus*
> innocuos vita *patientes* aetheris imi
> fecit et aeternos animam collegit in orbes:
> non illuc auro positi nec ture sepulti
> perveniunt.
>
>   (7-11)

There is an interesting inversion of terminology at line 371:

> at *impatiens virtus haerere* Catonis
> audet in ignotas agmen committere gentes.

Here *impatiens virtus haerere* means, in effect, *patientia*. And finally the term as it is regularly used in assessing the fertility of the land:[38]

> *impatiensque* solum Cereris cultore negato
> damnasti.
>
>   (857-858)

The *patientia* of the soil, its susceptibility for agricultural activities, is generally in an inverse relationship to the physical and moral *patientia* of its inhabitants.

By now it should be clear that Lucan, at a number of points throughout the ninth book of the *Pharsalia*, was concerned to present Cato in terms which recognizably equated him with the hardy primitive who appears both in the ethnographical tradition in general, and in Lucan's own ethnography of Libya. The description of that land, then, plays an integral role in the poet's artistic purpose. At the same time, the qualities with which Cato is invested are fully consonant with those possessed by the Stoic hero, the figure for which he is a virtual paradigm.

By investigating the possible sources from which Lucan drew in the ninth book, it will, I think, be possible to recover the essential nature of one area of Roman ethnography, and thereby to realize the full import of Lucan's construct. Such *Quellenforschung* is hardly new, and there is no need here for a full discussion of Lucan's models.[39] M. Wünsch has catalogued the most likely candidates: Livy for historical details, Strabo (4.1.7), Diodorus (5.26.1) and Seneca (*Quaest. Nat.* 2.6.4)[40] for the sandstorm. For geographical matters she posits Posidonius and Seneca as the probable sources.[41] The specific work of Seneca is the *de situ et sacris Aegyptiorum*, which is known only by title, but the title in itself is sufficient evidence that the treatise was an ethnography.[42]

Posidonian influence, with or without the mediation of Seneca, is quite plausible. Although it is rightly the trend now to regard this figure as less pervasively influential, in the area of geographical and ethnographical theory his importance is more generally accepted.[43] We can be virtually certain that Posidonius incorporated his Stoicism into his ethnographical studies; Athenaeus, before citing him on the dining habits of the Celts, noted:

> Ποσειδώνιος δὲ ὁ ἀπὸ τῆς Στοᾶς ἐν ταῖς Ἱστορίαις αἷς συνέθηκεν οὐκ ἀλλοτρίως ἧς προήρητο φιλοσοφίας πολλὰ πολλοῖς ἔθιμα καὶ νόμιμα ἀναγράφων ...
>
> (Athen. 4.151 e = Pos. fr. 67 Edel. and Kidd)[44]

A number of the fragments concern topics such as luxury among various nations,[45] or the effects of gold-mining on man's character.[46] And, even more relevant to our theme, he wrote in the following terms of the virtuous life of the early Italians:

> πάτριος μὲν γὰρ ἦν αὐτοῖς, ὥς φησι Ποσειδώνιος, καρτερία καὶ λιτὴ δίαιτα καὶ τῶν ἄλλων τῶν ὑπὸ τὴν κτῆσιν ἀφελὴς καὶ ἀπερίεργος χρῆσις, ἔτι δὲ εὐσέβεια μὲν θαυμαστὴ περὶ τὸ δαιμόνιον, δικαιοσύνη δὲ καὶ πολλὴ τοῦ πλημμελεῖν εὐλάβεια πρὸς πάντας ἀνθρώπους μετὰ τῆς κατὰ γεωργίαν ἀσκήσεως.
>
> (Athen. 6.274 a = fr. 266 Edel. and Kidd)

Here, then, associated with a less civilized race, are the traditional Stoic values, the same features with which Lucan endowed Cato: *duritia* (καρτερία), frugality, indifference towards material possessions, and a high sense of justice. From all of this it is quite clear that Posidonian ethnography must have been inextricably tied to Stoic ethics.

Whether Lucan was influenced by Posidonius' ethnography or by that of Seneca is a question which will not be answered, and one which is in fact immaterial. Although we have no more than the title of Seneca's study, there can be little doubt that it dealt, like the treatments of Posidonius, with the cultural and ethical levels of the people under examination. Most probably, although this is speculation, Seneca found grounds for condemning the way of life of the Egyptians.[47] Whatever the precise nature of Posidonian or Senecan "Stoic" ethnography, potentially either of these figures could have provided Lucan with the material for his ethical ethnography of Libya. His own poetic contribution was to combine with such a traditional presentation the figure of Cato, at harmony with the environment in which he appears.

Having postulated this "Stoic" ethnography, we should return briefly to Horace and Virgil. An observation on Epistle 1.16 of Horace, the starting-point of this study, is particularly relevant. The second part of the poem, immediately following the ethnography of the Sabine farm, deals with Stoic ethics to a degree unparalleled in the poetry of Horace (17-19). The transition from the description of the farm to this material, moreover, has troubled some critics.[48] On these 60 lines, M. J. McGann noted:[49]

> The terms *sapiens bonusque* (20), *stulti* (24), *sapiens emendatusque* (30), and *vir bonus et sapiens* (73), the statement that the good hate sin because they

love virtue (52), and the passages which recall the paradoxes that all sins are equal (55f.) and that only the wise man is free (63ff.), all these elements give the epistle a strong flavour of the Stoicism of ἀρετή, κατορθώματα and the σοφός and set it apart from the rest of the book...

Incidentally, included in the image of the *vir bonus* of these lines is his implicit *patientia*:

> vir bonus et sapiens audebit dicere 'Pentheu,
> rector Thebarum, quid me perferre *patique*
> indignum coges?'
>
>   (*Epist.* 1.16.73-74)[50]

It may be, then, that Horace, like Lucan, although in different ways, was also drawing on Posidonian or "Stoic" ethnography, and that the 'two parts' of *Epistle* 1.16 are to be seen in this light; Horace adopted a heavily Stoic stance in a poem which used a tradition (that of ethnography) whose elements had been incorporated into the ethical theory of that philosophy.

Yet Horace in this poem presented an environment which was beneficial. Such is the nature of Italy, and such was the nature of the poetic Italian countryside which had been largely his creation. However, there are qualifications to this which align his setting, in some ways, with the ethically ideal but hostile terrain of Lucan. For both are set apart from, and in contrast to the world of Rome and the world of modern agricultural civilization.[51] In both there is a simplicity of lifestyle which excludes the concerns of such civilization.

The same may be said of the landscapes of Virgil's *Georgics*, as we have seen them.[52] If there is a deliberate contrast between the advanced setting of the *laudes Italiae* and the simple success attained by the Corycian on his meagre plot, and if, as we have also claimed, both owe a formal and thematic debt to the ethnographical tradition, then Virgil's intent can be seen as related to that of Horace, and also as having affinities to the type of tradition from which Lucan drew. The old man of Tarentum had achieved self-sufficiency in a world explicitly set apart from the modern pursuits of Italian agriculture. His success, moreover, is in terms which are, not at all characteristically for Virgil, markedly Stoic:

> regum aequabat opes animis.
>
>   (*Geo.* 4.132)

NOTES

1. Notably N. Pinter, *Lucanus in tradendis rebus geographicis quibus usus sit auctoribus* (diss. Münster 1902); A. Bourgery, "La géographie dans Lucain", *RPh* 2 (1928) 25-40; L. Ekhardt, *Exkurse und Ekphraseis bei Lucan* (diss. Heidelberg 1936).

2. Not, however, on the ninth book. Most prominent is R. Nierhaus, "Zu den ethnographischen Angaben in Lukans Gallien-Exkurs", *Bonner Jahrb.* 153 (1953) 46-62.

3. Especially Pinter (above, n. 1) *passim*; so too R. Pichon, *Les Sources de Lucain* (Paris 1912) 34-42.

4. The description is in fact the only notable omission (apart from the more "poetical" instances with which we have been dealing) from Trüdinger's study. M. Wünsch's useful dissertation (*Lucan-Interpretation* [diss. Kiel 1930]), to which we shall refer later, identifies some parts of Lucan's treatment (46-49), although she is not fully aware of the actual tradition in which it is produced.

5. So Pinter (above, n. 1) 28-40; Bourgery (above, n. 1) 25, 29.

6. Ironically, the same attitude which pertains in most Virgilian scholarship, in regard to that poet's use of such description (see above, p. 35).

7. M. P. O. Morford, "The Purpose of Lucan's Ninth Book", *Latomus* 26 (1967) 123-129; "an unusual or exotic subject, however incidental to the main story, demands attention, and in this particular Lucan's rhetorical training asserts itself" (125). It is, I think, and so it will be argued in this chapter, a mistake to deny the possibility of meaning to poetry which draws from traditional material. For a similar attitude towards the account of Libya, see J. Aumont, "Caton en Libye", *REA* 70 (1968) 304-320.

8. The figure of Cato in the *Pharsalia* has, in general, evoked critical interest, but he has been studied in isolation, rather than in terms of the landscape in which he appears in the ninth book. Wünsch (above, n. 4, 49) is something of an exception to this trend. For the most recent study of Cato in this poem, see F. M. Ahl, *Lucan, An Introduction* (Ithaca and London 1976) Ch. 7, 231-271. In this chapter Ahl, although he sees Cato's actual march and the ordeal with the snakes as an indication of great *virtus*, does not examine the function of the actual description of Libya.

9. See Housman *ad* 9.413 for reference to geographers who deal with the question; notably Sall. *B.J.* 17.3 *plerique in parte tertia Africam posuere, pauci tantummodo Asiam et Europam esse, sed Africam in Europa.* Add to Housman's list Trog. 30.4.9 (*tertiam partem mundi*); Auson. *Epist.* 23 p. 267.22 Peiper; August. *Civ.* 16.17; see too Kurfess *ad* Sall. *B.J.* 17.3. Lucan appears to be the only author to posit a reason for viewing Africa as a part of Europe: the westerly wind blows from both these land masses, while the east wind derives from Asia.

10. Above, Ch. I, p. 17.

11. For every area with which he deals, Strabo gives the measurements; see 1.21 for his general treatment of the position of winds in geographical discussion.

12. In his ethnography of Britain, Tacitus employed a similar periphrasis to describe that country's climate: *asperitas frigorum abest* (*Agr.* 12.3).

13. This is clearly the force of *immotis* (437); see Housman *ad loc.*

14. Cf. Schroeder 31; it is, of course, particularly when accompanied by spontaneity, also a Utopian feature.

15. *Nulla putris radice tenetur* implies that grazing is altogether out of the question.

16. See above, Chapter II, p. 57.

17. Considering the similarity of theme and diction, as well as Lucan's general familiarity with Virgilian poetry, it is reasonable to suggest that this constitutes a deliberate reminiscence.

18. On this, see Schroeder 33.

19. So Ovid of the bronze age:

> itum est in viscera terrae,
> quasque recondiderat Stygiisque admoverat umbris,
> effodiuntur opes, irritamenta malorum.
> > (*Met.* 1.138-140)

20. Above, Chapter II, p. 57.

21. *Umbra* (428) is certainly correct over Bentley's *aura* ("aroma"). For Virgil and Horace this was also a feature of "non-civilized" ethnography: *ministrantem platanum potantibus umbras, Geo.* 4.146; *si quercus et ilex ... multa dominum iuvet umbra? Epist.* 1.16.9-10.

22. *Usus* is particularly pointed, for Virgil a feature of the world after the fall of Saturn, for Lucan the motivating force for the civilized Roman, in contrast to the primitive Nasamones.

23. This is a *topos* we have already met in Horace, *Odes* 3.24 (cf. above, pp. 54-5). Such contrast is familiar from Tacitean ethnography (see Gudeman on *Germ.* 5). Wünsch (above, n. 4, 48) has dealt to some extent with the theme in Lucan's lines.

24. On this, cf. above, Chapter IV, p. 98.

25. For other references, and for the conventional nature of this feature, see Schroeder 15-16.

26. As we shall see, *patientia*, a key element in ethnographical descriptions (cf. above, pp. 20-1), plays a crucial role in Lucan's ninth book.

27. It should be stressed that there seems to be no precedent for such a "digression" on Libya in the tradition of biographical treatments of Cato. Plutarch has a few lines on the march, with no account of the setting (*Cato* 56). Livy, as far as we can tell (*Perioch.* 112), had little more: *praeterea laboriosum M. Catonis in Africa per deserta cum legionibus iter.* Where ethnographies occurred in Livy, the epitomist seems to have indicated as much: *praeterea situm Galliarum continet* (*liber*), 103; *prima pars libri situm Germaniae moresque continet*, 104. In both of these books, Livy was doubtless heavily indebted to Caesar's ethnographical treatments. In general, the entire ninth book of Lucan, while eclectically traditional, is strikingly original. For a good demonstration of Lucan's manipulation and conversion of source material, see R. B. Kebric, "Lucan's Snake Episode (IX 587-937): A Historical Model", *Latomus* 35 (1976) 380-382.

28. Ahl (above, n. 8) 231; he also points out that the entry of Cato is delayed until the second book, both

to prevent interference with the portrayals of Caesar and Pompey, and to separate Cato from the two main protagonists. See too Ahl 239-252, for the Stoic *virtus* exemplified in Cato's speech to Brutus and in the account of his marriage to Marcia.

29. *ThLL* 7.29.73-76: "de hominibus (aut temporum priscorum, sc. heroibus et Romanorum maioribus, aut condicionis certae [de iuvenibus; de philosophis; de sacerdote; de gentibus exteris]...)". A common element of high morality can be seen to inform all these categories.

30. Cf. for example, the account of Plutarch (*Cato* 53).

31. R. G. M. Nisbet and M. Hubbard (A Commentary on Horace: *Odes* Book II [Oxford 1978]) *ad loc.*, following Bücheler and Kiessling and Heinze, see in Horace's *intonsi* a "contrast with the clipped shrubs of ornamental gardens". While such a view is possible, in that the word in its surface sense already carries a moral force, it does not seem altogether necessary.

32. For the importance of both these passages in the tradition of idealization of primitive societies (and for a demonstration of their thoroughly conventional nature), see A. Riese, *Die Idealisirung der Naturvölker des Nordens in der griechischen und römischen Literatur* (Frankfurt am Main 1875) 26-28. This invaluable study also includes Lucan (33-34), but only those passages treating northern barbarians (1.458-462, 7.432-436, 8.363-364).

33. Above, Chapter IV, pp. 98-9.

34. Similarly see *de const.* 15.4 *patientia laborum*; *ad Marc.* 2.3 *Stoicam duritiam.*

35. Seneca did refer briefly to Cato's *patientia*: *vides posse homines* laborem pati: *per medias Africae solitudines pedes duxit exercitum* (*Epist.* 104.33). Of course he may by this time have had the benefit of Lucan's treatment; obviously at some point, and certainly after publication of the ninth book, Cato's march became paradigmatic.

36. *Mollitia*, of course, both in ethnographical and Stoic contexts, is precisely the opposite of *duritia*, or *patientia*.

37. I have accepted Heinsius' *limite* over MS *milite*, mainly on the force of recent argument by L. H°kanson, "Problems in Lucan's De Bello Civili", *Proc. Camb. Philol. Soc.* 25 (1979) 48. He seems quite correct in pointing out that *duro* in no way suits *milite* in the present context. Additionally, it may be noted, *limite* leaves the focus on Cato, which is the point of other references to *duritia* in the ninth book.

38. Tacitus was to use the term in this sense in his ethnographies of Britain (*patiens frugum, Agr.* 12.5) and Germany (*terra ... frugiferarum arborum impatiens, Germ.* 5.1).

39. Chiefly see Pinter (above, n. 1) 28-40; Wünsch (above, n. 4) 57-58.

40. With Seneca as the most likely and accessible of the three.

41. Wünsch (above, n. 4) 49; again, Seneca is suggested as the intermediary.

42. For the title, see Servius *ad Aen.* 6.154; cf. Norden, *Die germanische Urgeschichte* 451-454, for evidence that this work would have constituted an ethnographical study. Seneca also appears to have

written such an account of India (*Seneca etiam apud nos temptata Indiae commentatione...* Plin. *N.H.* 6.60).

43. Norden (*Die germanische Urgeschichte*, especially Ch. 2, "Quellenkritisches zur Ethnographie europäischer Völker") has put Posidonian influence beyond doubt. A clear, but more restricted, demonstration is made by G. Rudberg, *Forschungen zu Poseidonios*, Skrifter utgifna af K. Humanistika Vetenskaps-Samfundet i Uppsala 20.3 (1918) 73-87.

44. This fragment is from the *Histories*, but from what follows the context is clearly of a purely ethnographical nature.

45. Fragments 58, 59, 62a, 62b, 64 Edel. and Kidd.

46. Fragment 240a Edel. and Kidd.

47. As Pompeius Trogus, in comparing them with the Scythians, relates: *et quanto Scythis sit caelum asperius quam Aegyptiis, tanto et corpora et ingenia duriora, ap.* Just. 2.1.13.

48. On this matter, see above, Chapter 1, n. 33.

49. *Studies in Horace's First Book of Epistles*, Collection Latomus 100 (1969) 74-75.

50. See above, Chapter I, p. 20, for Horace's (albeit humorous) claim that he possesses *patientia*: *rure meo possum quidvis perferre patique, Epist.* 1.15.17.

51. On this feature of Horace's landscapes, cf. above, Chapter I, pp. 13-14. Both the Utopia of the Sixteenth Epode and the Sabine farm of *Epistle* 1.16 are depicted in separation from Rome *and* civilized concerns.

52. Above, Chapter II, pp. 57-60.

VI. TACITUS: THE TRADITION MATURED

The preceding chapter exposed an apparent contradiction in the tradition with which we have been dealing. Horace's ethically ideal landscape was one whose features were characterized by balance and harmony. For Lucan, on the other hand, and for the line of ethnographical development from which he drew, the precise opposite obtained: Cato's *virtus* existed and was promoted in a setting which was depicted in the harshest and most extreme terms. Particularly under the category of climate, this distinction appears most forcefully; Horace's farm is ideal (*temperiem laudes, Epist.* 1.16.8), Lucan's Libya a desolate waste (*temperies vitalis abest*, 9.435). The two environments, then, physically in complete contrast, both operate as ethically positive settings, the exclusive arenas for (predominantly Stoic) *virtus*.

It is fairly clear that Lucan's outlook is, from an ethnographical standpoint, the more 'correct'. This emerges from his adherence to the traditional sources. In this matter it is the treatment of Horace which was idiosyncratic, for he was faced with a dilemma. As was demonstrated in the first chapter, he came throughout his poetic career to view, or at least to present, the landscape of his Sabine farm as the only viable setting. He set it, moreover, in contrast to the developed and debased world of civilization. And yet this farm was a part of Italy, and Italy, beyond other lands, has a positive climate, great productivity, and all the marks of civilization. Horace's solution, particularly in *Epistle* 1.16, was to deny to his farm the existence of such productivity, and to replace it with a more individual, virtually golden age, spontaneity of produce.[1] This, moreover, at the cost of deliberately disavowing the presence of items which obviously flourished on his farm, and which in an earlier poem (*Epist.* 1.14) he had in fact claimed for it.[2] So too, Virgil's wholly positive Italian setting in the *Georgics* – the old man's plot (4.125-148) – was expressly without civilized agricultural activity, and it was thereby distinguished from the civilized Italy of the *laudes Italiae*.[3]

Perhaps the best commentary on this dichotomy, and in many ways the full potential of the ethnographical tradition (in prose or poetry), is to be recovered from the works of the greatest exponent of the genre, Tacitus.

The works of Tacitus have, of course, already formed an essential part of our study, in that the *Agricola* and *Germania* represent the fullest and most careful treatments of the tradition. The position of Tacitus is central, best defined by Norden,[4] who, in his exhaustive examination of the *Germania*, established this author in an ethnographical genealogy traceable back through Posidonius in particular to the beginnings of the tradition. These two works, especially the latter,

prospect – to imply a savage contrast".[22] It is the nature of this contrast that requires further attention. We have already seen that the island is specified as a *locus amoenus* (*peramoena*). Also that in this, and in its *temperies*, it is depicted in terms extremely close to those used by Horace of his Sabine farm. But while for Horace such perfection was the setting for the *vir bonus*, for Tacitus the complete opposite applies: *luxus* and *malum otium* thrive in a physically benign environment.

This apparent contradiction exposes the divergence and the originality of the Augustan attitude. For it is Tacitus' scheme which is in line with traditional ethnographical theory. Just as a harsh environment produces hardy and morally superior inhabitants (as we saw in the case of Lucan's Libya), so the ideal and balanced environment theoretically breeds a race lacking in fortitude and with a low moral worth. This was a part of the tradition at least as far back as the Hippocratic treatise, *Airs, Waters, Places*:

περὶ δὲ τῆς ἀθυμίας τῶν ἀνθρώπων καὶ τῆς ἀνανδρείης, ὅτι ἀπολεμώτεροί εἰσι τῶν Εὐρωπαίων οἱ ᾿Ασιηνοὶ καὶ ἡμερώτεροι τὰ ἤθεα αἱ ὧραι αἴτιαι μάλιστα, οὐ μεγάλας τὰς μεταβολὰς ποιεύμεναι οὔτε ἐπὶ τὸ θερμὸν οὔτε ἐπὶ τὸ ψυχρόν, ἀλλὰ παραπλησίως.

(Hipp. *aer.* 16)[23]

Somewhat closer to Tacitus, a passage from Pompeius Trogus is particularly illuminating:

ac sic gens industria quondam potens et manu strenua effeminata *mollitie luxuriaque virtutem* pristinam *perdidit* et quos ante Cyrum invictos bella praestiterunt, in *luxuriam* lapsos *otium* ac *desidia* superavit.

(Iust. 1.7.13)[24]

Here the emphasis is not so much on a permanent state as on a decline which comes upon a society, but in that the subjects are a traditionally weak people, Asiatics, the similarities of diction between their moral condition and that of Tiberius in his *locus amoenus* do seem significant. Tacitus himself, in an ethnographical context, applied this same terminology to the Gauls (in contrast to the unconquered Britons):

nam Gallos quoque in bellis floruisse accepimus; mox *segnitia* cum *otio* intravit, *amissa virtute* pariter ac libertate. quod Britannorum olim victis evenit: ceteri manent quales Galli fuerunt.

(*Agr.* 11.4)

Capreae, then, is presented, through ethnographical detail, as a separable and distinct land, physically and climatically ideal. Appropriately, its occupant, Tiberius, manifests the same characteristics (*luxus et malum otium*) as in ethnographical accounts (Tacitean and other) are exhibited by inhabitants of areas which are either physically ideal or have been exposed to civilized influences. As for society in general, so for the individual, environment is seen as having a profound effect on ethical outlook.[25] We have examined the attitudes of Horace and Virgil to this complex. To these attitudes Lucan and particularly Tacitus, the most highly literary author in the tradition of prose ethnography, provide a commentary. The world of Augustus had passed, and with it the need (and perhaps the desire) for ambiguity in such matters. The harsh Libyan desert could be implicitly praised as the breeding-ground for *patientia* and Stoic *virtus*. Germany, with its primitive simplicity, could be viewed favourably and in contrast to Rome, with her pursuit of *luxuria* and declining morality. And, ultimately, ambivalence towards one's own society, in the case of civilized Italy permitted – even required – by traditional geographical and ethnographical theory, could now be openly expressed, as the tradition asserted itself.

NOTES

1. See above, Chapter I, pp. 12-14.

2. M. J. McGann (*Studies in Horace's First Book of Epistles*, Coll. Latomus 100 [1969] 74) notes the difference, without elaboration: "there is an air of stillness about the farm of *Epi.* 16".

3. Cf. above, Chapter II, pp. 57-8.

4. *Die germanische Urgeschichte, passim*; for a graphic indication of the position of Posidonius, see the "stemma" on p. 170.

5. In addition to the studies of Trüdinger and Norden, and the commentaries on both the *Agricola* (chiefly Ogilvie and Richmond) and the *Germania* (Much, and Anderson), cf. also E. Wolff, "Das geschichtliche Verstehen in Tacitus Germania", *Hermes* 69 (1934) 121-166.

6. The works of Trüdinger, Norden and particularly Schroeder (on ethnographical *topoi*), in demonstrating the literary tradition to which the monograph belongs, have countered such extreme views of the *Germania*. For this shift in critical attitude, see Anderson (above, n. 5) ix-xix.

7. Anderson ix. The discrepancy between the two halves of Tacitus' study is rather puzzling; could it be that the first part was produced before 96, with moral criticism applying to Domitian's Rome, the second half being written under a sense of greater optimism, after the accession of Trajan?

8. Juvenal 5 provides a good elaboration of this *topos* on the reciprocity of service in a debased patron-client relationship.

9. For a discussion of this passage see Norden, *Die germanische Urgeschichte* 110-115.

10. So R. Syme, *Tacitus* II (Oxford 1958) 730.

11. The only category omitted, not surprisingly perhaps, is that of agricultural produce.

12. So Pliny, in his brief account of the islands off the Italian coast: *mox a Surrento VIII distantes Tiberi principis arce nobiles Capreae circuitu XI, N.H.* 3.82.

13. The word *importuosus*, whose Greek equivalent (ἀλίμενος) is found in an ethnographical context (*Peripl. M. Eux.* 37), occurs elsewhere in the same setting: Livy 10.2.4; Mela 1.37, Pliny, *N.H.* 4.73; elsewhere in Tacitus: *Ann.* 12.20. Syme (above, n. 10, 730) characterizes it as Sallustian. So E. Koestermann (*C. Sallustius Crispus, Bellum Iugurthinum* [Heidelberg 1971] 89) on this Tacitean instance: "sein Vorbild ist offenbar Sallust".

14. He avoided completely the more common prose variants (*temperatio, temperatura*). The other instance of *temperies* is at *Ann.* 4.55.4, in the reporting of a letter describing the benefits of Lydia; here, too, the setting seems to be ethnographical: *ubertatemque fluminum suorum, temperiem caeli ac dites circum terras memorabat.*

15. In this avoidance of commonplace, he is perhaps close to Virgil (cf. above, Chapter II, pp. 40-1).

16. Above, Chapter I, pp. 10-11.

17. Above, Chapter I, p. 17; the importance of the Tacitean instance will be discussed shortly.

18. For the use of the verb *tenere* (or *habere*) in such accounts, see above, Chapter IV, n. 15.

19. In this respect, Tacitus' intention is much like that of Virgil in his description of the old man of Tarentum as a Corycian (see above, Chapter II, p. 56).

20. The sequence suggests that this is the light in which we are to view Tiberius; Tacitus first treats the original inhabitants (Greeks and Teleboeans), then immediately presents the present occupant: *sed tum Tiberius ... insederat*. The manner is close to that of Sallust's Libyan ethnography (*Africam initio habuere Gaetuli et Libyes ... sed postquam ... B.J.* 18) as well as to Virgil's Roman typology (*haec nemora indigenae Fauni Nymphaeque tenebant ... tum manus Ausonia ... tum reges ... Aen.* 8.314-332).

21. J. P. V. D. Balsdon (*JRS* 36 [1946] 168) in a review of D. M. Pippidi, *Autour de Tibère* (Bucharest 1944), the relevant chapter of which ("Tacite et Tibère") is somewhat more accessible in *Ephemeris Dacoromana* 8 (1938) 233-297. Of course other events (the deaths of Livia and Sejanus) can also be seen as contributing to the deterioration of Tiberius' character.

22. *Tacitus* I (Oxford 1958) 349.

23. This is the same passage which Virgil appears to have contradicted in the *laudes Italiae* (cf. above, Chapter II, pp. 40-1).

24. We have already observed *otium* as a feature of primitive societies; there it is of the more positive type (see Schroeder 16-18). As in general, so in an ethnographical context, the term is thoroughly ambivalent. On the divergent senses held by this word, see A. J. Woodman, "Some Implications of *otium* in Catullus 51.13-16", *Latomus* 25 (1966) 217-226.

25. In this connection, it is of interest that for Sallust, in style and diction, the biographical notice has affinities to the category on *gentes* in ethnography. First consider him on Catiline: *corpus patiens inediae*

algoris vigiliae (*B. C.* 5.3); then on the Libyans: *genus hominum salubri corpore, velox, patiens laborum* (*B.J.* 17.6). In both passages, Sallust adopts an abbreviated, summary style. The same style was adopted by Livy in his depiction of Hannibal: *caloris ac frigoris patientia par; cibi potionisque desiderio naturali, non voluptate modus finitus; vigiliarum somnique nec die nec nocte discriminata tempora ...* (21.4).

CONCLUSION

We have been examining the artistic application and manipulation (in both poetry and prose) of an enduring technical tradition, fixed in diction and form. In the process it has emerged that such material, originally outside the scope of the poetic experience, was, at the hands of learned poets, transformed and instilled with a significance which transcends that of the technical tradition; through this poeticising the tradition itself was elevated. Moreover, for Virgil and Horace in particular, ethnography may be seen as a vehicle for the expression of views whose full implications can be recovered only through familiarity with that tradition – again the stamp of learned poetry.

With the notable exception of Lucretius, whose scientific and philosophical tendencies led him to a preference for theories of cultural improvement, the Roman attitude towards cultural change (at least the literary attitude) is predominantly primitivistic; society is essentially in a state of unremitting decline:

> aetas parentum peior avis tulit
> nos nequiores, mox daturos
> progeniem vitiosiorem.

(Hor. Odes 3.6.46-48)

Such sentiment, moreover, finds expression as much in the historians as in the poets. The early works of Virgil and Horace are in accord with this movement. Where societal issues are confronted (e.g., *Ecl.* 4; *Epds.* 7, 16), the resulting poetry is one of escape. The dreadful reality of the civil wars – the historical demonstration of decline for the early Augustan poets – finds its resolution in constructs of the imagination (the return to a golden age, or migration to the *beatae insulae*), and solutions emerge which are no solution at all, but merely fanciful answers to the insoluble problem of decline.

It has been our contention that Actium and the consolidation of the Augustan régime did not produce in these poets a total reversal in cultural outlook, that, in spite of some blatant dicta to the contrary, the Augustan era was not perceived simply as a return of the golden age to Latium. Doubts about the quality of civilization continued, and one of the ways in which they were expressed was through judgement against the theories of the ethnographical tradition. Such abstraction became necessary as, through the thirties, Virgil and Horace found themselves under the patronage of the new ruler's first minister. The expression of these doubts, then, was on a deeper and more ambiguous level. This is not to suggest that Augustan poetry is an arcane construct, produced by hypocritical subversives, but by the same token it seems reasonably clear that the genuine relief attended by *pax Augusta* was tempered with a continuing uneasiness, existing *outside* any specific political issues, and thoroughly in line with traditional Roman thought.

For Horace, as we have shown, the answer lay in many ways in a rejection of the very terms of nation and society. His development of the landscape of his Sabine farm represented a retreat, this time a more realistic one, from the public world into that of poetry and the country – to the exclusion of the city and what it stood for:

> parvum parva decent: mihi iam non regia Roma
> sed vacuum Tibur placet aut imbelle Tarentum.
> (*Epist.* 1.7.44-45)

His own Italy and the successful Italian setting of Virgil, these are the alternatives. The Sixteenth Epistle, containing his ethnographical description of this world, confirms this separation and presents the poet's new environment in exclusive terms as a private, individualistic setting.

Virgil, the profounder poet, remained within the terms of national and social experience. In the *Georgics* in particular we see his need to confront the realities of the world of civilization. The golden age has passed, and he acknowledges as much (1.121-149). What replaces it, the world of *labor*, for various reasons is flawed. Where success is possible, it is in association with a limited, again individualistic, world (that of the old man of Tarentum), flourishing precisely in terms which exclude the activities of civilized agrarian man. And here, as we might expect, the setting is closest to that of Horace. On the other hand, where we might expect unqualified approval from an enthusiastic supporter of the new age (e.g. in the *laudes Italiae*), Virgil's alterations and extensions of the tradition from which he was drawing seem to imply an ambivalence, and to suggest misgivings about the quality of the society depicted.

A new dimension was reached with Lucan and Tacitus. For them ethnographical theory asserted its true system of values, particularly as it was applied to Libya and Germany. In the works of both of these authors the deficiencies of a technological society emerge either implicitly or explicitly, as a contrast is drawn between the primitive and the advanced. In this process the ambiguity which was necessarily so much a part of the Augustan attitude diminished, and straightforward application of a technical, scientific tradition stood to assert the conventional values of primitivism.

This study has drawn only from a single tradition, but the point should be clear: if we can, with assurance, identify and characterize elements of traditions originally outside the poetic range, and observe the poetic extensions and distortions of such traditions, then we will be better equipped to understand that poetry, and to do justice to the learning, allusiveness and ambiguity which are the property of great poets.

WORKS CITED

Abbreviations

Altevogt

Altevogt, H. *Labor Improbus, Eine Vergilstudie*, Orbis Antiquus 8 (1952).

Conington

Conington, J. P. *P. Vergili Maronis Opera*, 5th ed. revised by H. Nettleship, vol. 1 (London 1898).

Norden, *Die germanische Urgeschichte*

Norden, E. *Die germanische Urgeschichte in Tacitus Germania*, 4th ed. (Stuttgart 1959).

Ogilvie and Richmond

Ogilvie, R. M. and Richmond, I. *Cornelii Taciti De Vita Agricolae* (Oxford 1967).

Otis

Otis, B. *Virgil, A Study in Civilized Poetry* (Oxford 1963).

Richter

Richter, W. *Vergil, Georgica*, Das Wort der Antike 5 (1957).

Schroeder

Schroeder, A. *De Ethnographiae Antiquae locis quibusdam communibus Observationes* (diss. Halle 1921).

Trüdinger

Trüdinger, K. *Studien zur Geschichte der griechisch-römischen Ethnographie* (diss. Basel 1918).

FGH

Die Fragmente der griechischen Historiker, ed. F. Jacoby (Leiden 1954-1969).

ThLL

Thesaurus Linguae Latinae (Leipzig 1900-).

Ahl, F. M. *Lucan, An Interpretation* (Ithaca and London 1976).

Anderson, J. G. C. *Cornelii Taciti De Origine et Situ Germanorum* (Oxford 1938).

Aumont, J. "Caton en Libye", *REA* 70 (1968) 304-320.

Axelson, B. *Unpoetische Wörter, Ein Beitrag zur Kenntnis der lateinischen Dichtersprache*, Skrifter Utgivna av Vetenskaps-Societeten i Lund 29 (1945).

Badian, E. *Roman Imperialism in the Late Republic*, 2nd ed. (Oxford 1968).

Baldry, H. C. *The Unity of Mankind in Greek Thought* (Cambridge 1965).

Balsdon, J. P. V. D. rev. of D. M. Pippidi, *Autour de Tibère*, in *JRS* 36 (1946) 168-173.

Becker, C. *Das Spätwerk des Horaz* (Göttingen 1963).

Beckmann, F. *Geographie und Ethnographie in Caesars Bellum Gallicum* (Dortmund 1930).

Binder, G. *Aeneas und Augustus, Interpretationem zum 8. Buch der Aeneis*, Beitr. zur klass. Philol. 38 (1971).

Borzsák, I. "Von Hippokrates bis Vergil", in *Vergiliana*, ed. H. Bardon and R. Verdière (Leiden 1971) 41-55.

Bourgery, A. "La géographie dans Lucain", *RPh* 2 (1928) 25-40.

Bovie, S. P. "The Imagery of Ascent-Descent in Vergil's *Georgics*", *AJP* 77 (1956) 337-358.

Brind' amour, P. "Paulum silvae super his foret", *REA* 74 (1972) 86-93.

Buchheit, V. *Vergil über die Sendung Roms*, Gymnasium Beihefte 3 (1963).

Burck, E. *De Vergili Georgicon Partibus Iussivis* (diss. Leipzig 1926).

———— "Die Komposition von Vergils Georgika", *Hermes* 64 (1929) 279-321 = *Vom Menschenbild in der Römischen Literatur* (Heidelberg 1966) 89-116.

———— "Der korykische Greis in Vergils Georgica", in *Navicula Chilonensis* (Leiden 1956) 156-172 = *Vom Menschenbild* 117-129.

Burton, A. *Diodorus Siculus, Book 1, A Commentary* (Leiden 1972).

Canter, H. V. "Praise of Italy in Ancient Authors", *CJ* 33 (1938) 457-470.

Cattin, A. "La Géographie dans les Tragédies de Sénèque", *Latomus* 22 (1963) 685-703.

Clausen, W. V. "An Interpretation of the *Aeneid*", *HSCP* 68 (1964) 139-147.

Cole, T. *Democritus and the Sources of Greek Anthropology*, APhA Monographs 25 (1967).

Commager, S. *The Odes of Horace* (New Haven 1962).

Dahlmann, H. "Vates", *Philologus* 97 (1948) 337-353 = *Kleine Schriften*, Collectanea 19 (1970) 35-51.

———— *Der Bienenstaat in Vergils Georgica*, Akad. der Wiss. und der Lit. Mainz, Abhand. Geistes- und Sozialwiss. Klasse 10 (1954) = *Kleine Schriften* 181-196.

D'Arms, J. H. *Romans on the Bay of Naples* (Cambridge, Mass. 1970).

Deratini, N. "Virgile et l'âge d'or", *RPh* 5 (1931) 128-131.

Dihle, A. "Zur Hellenistischen Ethnographie", in *Grecs et Barbares*, Entretiens Fond. Hardt 8 (1961) 205-239.

Dobson, J. F. "The Posidonius Myth", *CQ* 12 (1918) 179-195.

Earl, D. C. *The Political Thought of Sallust* (Cambridge 1961).

Ekhardt, L. *Exkurse und Ekphraseis bei Lucan* (diss. Heidelberg 1936).

Enk, P. J. *Sex. Propertii Elegiarum Liber Secundus* (Leiden 1961).

Fischer, R. *Das ausseritalische geographische Bild in Vergils Georgica, in den Oden des Horaz und in den Elegien des Properz* (diss. Zürich 1968).

Fraenkel, E. *Horace* (Oxford 1957).

Frentz, W. *Mythologisches in Vergils Georgica*, Beitr. zur klass. Philol. 21 (1967).

Garn, E. *Odenelemente im 1. Epistelbuch des Horaz* (diss. [microfilm] Freiburg i. Br. 1954).

Geffcken, J. "Saturnia Tellus", *Hermes* 27 (1892) 381-388.

George, E. V. *Aeneid VIII and the Aitia of Callimachus*, Mnemos. Suppl. 27 (1974).

Gissinger, F. "Meropis", *RE* 15 (1931) 1056-1065.

Gomme, A. W. and Sandbach, F. H. *Menander, A Commentary* (Oxford 1973).

Gossen, H. and Steier, A. "Krebs", *RE* 11 (1922) 1663-1690.

Gow, A. S. F. and Scholfield, A. F. *Nicander* (Cambridge 1953).

Graf, E. "Ad aureae aetatis fabulam symbola", *Leipz. Stud.* 8 (1885) 1-84.

Griffin, J. "Augustan Poetry and the Life of Luxury", *JRS* 66 (1976) 87-105.

———— "The Fourth *Georgic*, Virgil, and Rome", *GR* 26 (1979) 61-80.

Håkanson, L. "Problems in Lucan's De Bello Civili", *PCPhS* 25 (1979) 26-51.

Heinze, R. *Virgils Epische Technik*, 3rd ed. (Leipzig 1915).

Herrmann, L. "Le Quatrième Livre des Géorgiques et les Abeilles d'Actium", *REA* 33 (1931) 219-224.

Highet, G. *The Speeches of Vergil's Aeneid* (Princeton 1972).

Horsfall, N. "Numanus Remulus: Ethnography and Propaganda in *Aen.,* ix, 598ff.," *Latomus* 30 (1971) 1108-1116.

Immerwahr, H. R. *Form and Thought in Herodotus*, APhA Monographs 23 (1966).

Jacoby, F. "Herodotus", *RE* Suppl. 2 (1913) 205-520.

Jessen, O. "Argonautai", *RE* 2 (1895) 743-787.

Johnson, W. R. *Darkness Visible, A Study of Vergil's Aeneid* (Berkeley and Los Angeles 1976).

Kebric, R. B. "Lucan's Snake Episode (IX 587-937): A Historical Model", *Latomus* 35 (1976) 380-382.

Keller, O. *Epilegomena zu Horaz* III (Leipzig 1880 [repr. Hildesheim 1976]).

Kiessling, A. *Q. Horatius Flaccus Briefe*, 4th ed. revised by R. Heinze (Berlin 1914).

Klingner, F. *Virgils Georgica*, Bibl. der Alten Welt, Forschung und Deutung (Zürich 1963).

Klotz, A. "Geographie und Ethnographie in Caesars *Bellum Gallicum*", *RhM* 83 (1934) 66-96.

Koenen, L. "Papyrology in the Federal Republic of Germany and Fieldwork of the International Photographic Archive in Cairo", *Studia Papyrologica* 15 (1976) 39-79.

Koestermann, E. *C. Sallustius Crispus, Bellum Iugurthinum* (Heidelberg 1971).

Krappe, A. H. "A Source of Vergil, *Georg.* II. 136-76", *CQ* 20 (1926) 42-44.

Krauss, F. B. *An Interpretation of the Omens, Portents and Prodigies recorded by Livy, Tacitus and Suetonius* (diss. Univ. of Pennsylvania 1930).

Kroll, W. "Nikandros", *RE* 17 (1936) 250-265.

Laffranque, M. *Poseidonios d'Apamée* (Paris 1964).

La Penna, A. "Sallustio, *Hist.* II 83M", *RFIC* 99 (1971), 61-62.

Leach, E. W. "*Sedes Apibus:* From the *Georgics* to the *Aeneid*", *Vergilius* 23 (1977) 2-16.

Lovejoy, A. O. and Boas, G. *Primitivism and Related Ideas in Antiquity* (Baltimore, 1935 [repr. New York 1965]).

Lünenborg, J. *Das philosophische Weltbild in Vergils Georgika* (diss Münster 1935).

Lugli, G. "La villa sabina d'Orazio", *MAAL* 31 (1926) 457-598.

McGann, M. J. "The Sixteenth Epistle of Horace", *CQ* n.s. 10 (1960) 205-212.

———— *Studies in Horace's First Book of Epistles*, Coll. Latomus 100 (1969).

Martin, R. "Virgile et la Scythie", *REL* 44 (1966) 286-304.

Meuli, K. "Scythica Vergiliana, Ethnographisches, Archäologisches und Mythologisches zu Vergils *Georkika* 3, 367ff.", *Schweiz. Archiv für Volkskunde* 56 (1960) 88-200.

Mirsch, P. "De M. Ter. Varronis antiquitatum rerum humanarum libris XXV", *Leipz. Stud.* 5 (1882) 1-144.

Morford, M. P. O. "The Purpose of Lucan's Ninth Book", *Latomus* 26 (1967) 123-129.

Müller, K. E. *Geschichte der Antiken Ethnographie und Ethnologischen Theoriebildung, Von den Anfängen bis auf die Byzantinischen Historiographen* I, Stud. zur Kulturkunde 29 (1972).

Newman, J. K. *Augustus and the New Poetry*, Coll. Latomus 88 (1967).

———— *The Concept of Vates in Augustan Poetry*, Coll. Latomus 89 (1967).

Nierhaus, R. "Zu den Ethnographischen Angaben in Lukans Gallien-Exkurs", Bonner Jahrb. 153 (1953) 46-62.

Nisbet, R. G. M. and Hubbard, M. *A Commentary on Horace: Odes Book II* (Oxford 1978).

Norden, E. "Beiträge zur Geschichte der griechischen Philosophie", *Jahrb. für class. Philol.* Suppl. 19 (1893) 365-462.

———— *P. Vergilius Maro Aeneis Buch VI*, 4th ed. (Stuttgart 1957).

Ogilvie, R. M. *A Commentary on Livy Books 1-5* (Oxford 1965).

Olck, "Biene", *RE* 3 (1897) 431-450.

———— "Eiche", *RE* 5 (1905) 2013-2076.

Paratore, E. *Introduzione alle Georgiche* (Palermo 1938).

Parry, A. A. "The Two Voices of Vergil's *Aeneid*", *Arion* 2 (1963) 66-80.

Perkell, C. *Pessimism in the Georgics of Virgil* (diss. Harvard 1977).

Perret, J. *Virgile, l'homme et l'oeuvre* (Paris 1952).

Pfligersdorffer, G. *Studien zu Poseidonios*, SitzBer. Oest. Akad. der Wiss., phil.-hist. Klasse 232.5 (1959).

Pichon, R. *Les Sources de Lucain* (Paris 1912).

Pinter, N. *Lucanus in tradendis rebus geographicis quibus usus sit auctoribus* (diss. Münster 1902).

Pippidi, D. M. "Tacite et Tibère", *Ephemeris Dacoromana* 8 (1938) 233-297 = *Autour de Tibère* (Bucharest 1944) 11ff.

Pöhlmann, R. von *Geschichte der sozialen Frage und des Sozialismus in der Antiken Welt* II, 3rd ed. (Munich 1925).

Pohlenz, M. *Die Stoa, Geschichte einer geistigen Bewegung*, 2 vols. 2nd ed. (Göttingen 1959).

Pucci, P. "Horace's Banquet in *Odes* 1.17", *TAPhA* 105 (1975) 259-281.

Putnam, M. C. J. *The Poetry of the Aeneid* (Cambridge, Mass. 1965).

———— "Italian Virgil and the Idea of Rome", in *Janus, Essays in Ancient and Modern Studies* (Ann Arbor 1975).

———— *The Georgics: Virgil's Poem of the Earth* (Princeton 1979).

Quinn, K. *Virgil's Aeneid, A Critical Description* (London 1968).

Rehm, B. *Das geographische Bild des alten Italien in Vergils Aeneis*, Philologus Suppl. 24.2 (1932).

Reinhardt, K. "Poseidonios", *RE* 22 (1953) 558-826.

Reynen, H. "Klima und Krankheit auf den Inseln der Seligen", *Gymnasium Beihefte* 4 (1964) 77-104.

———— "Ewiger Frühling und goldene Zeit, Zum Mythos des goldenen Zeitalters bei Ovid und Vergil", *Gymnasium* 72 (1965) 415-433.

Riese, A. *Die Idealisirung der Naturvölker des Nordens in der griechischen und römischen Literatur* (Frankfurt am Main 1875).

Rohde, E. *Der griechische Roman und seine Vorläufer*, 3rd ed. (Leipzig 1914).

Ross, D. O. *Backgrounds to Augustan Poetry: Gallus, Elegy and Rome* (Cambridge 1975).

Rothstein, M. *Die Elegien des Sextus Propertius* I (Berlin 1898).

Rudberg, G. *Forschungen zu Poseidonios* (Uppsala 1918).

St Denis, E. de "Une Source de Virgile dans les Géorgiques", *REL* 16 (1938) 297-317.

Schmidt, E. A. "Das horazische Sabinum als Dichterlandschaft", *Antike und Abendland* 23 (1977) 97-112.

Schönbeck, G. *Der locus amoenus von Homer bis Horaz* (diss. Heidelberg 1962).

Schulten, "Sertorius", *RE* 2A (1923) 1746-1753.

Schweizer, H. J. *Vergil und Italien* (diss. Zürich 1967).

Snell, B. "Die 16. Epode von Horaz und Vergils 4. Ekloge", *Hermes* 73 (1938) 237-242.

Spoerri, W. "Zu Diodor von Sizilien 1, 7/8", *MH* 18 (1961) 63-82.

Suerbaum, W. "Aeneas zwischen Troja und Rom, Zur Funktion der Genealogie und der Ethnographie in Vergils Aeneis", *Poetica* 1 (1967) 176-204.

Syme, R. *Tacitus*, 2 vols. (Oxford 1958).

———— *Sallust* (Berkeley and Los Angeles 1964).

Tarn, W. W. "Alexander, Cynics and Stoics", *AJP* 60 (1939) 41-70.

Taylor, M. E. "Primitivism in Virgil", *AJP* 76 (1955) 261-278.

Thomas, R. F. "L. Lucullus' Triumphal Agnomen", *AJAH* 2 (1977) 172.

Tierney, J. J. "The Celtic Ethnography of Posidonius", *Proc. Royal Irish Acad.* 60, Sect. C (1960) 189-275.

Tiffon, E. "Salluste et la géographie", in *Littérature gréco-romaine et géographie historique*, Mélanges Dion, ed. R. Chevallier (Paris 1974).

Tränkle, H. *Die Sprachkunst des Properz und die Tradition der lateinischen Dichtersprache*, Hermes Einzelschriften 15 (1960).

Troxler-Keller, I. *Die Dichterlandschaft des Horaz* (Heidelberg 1964).

Voit, L. "Das Sabinum im 16. Brief des Horaz", *Gymnasium* 82 (1975) 412-426.

Wieland, H. *Ut currat sententia – Beobachtungen zur Bewegungsführung in den Satiren und Episteln des Horaz* (diss. Freiburg i. Br. 1950).

Wiesen, D. S. "The Pessimism of the Eighth Aeneid", *Latomus* 32 (1973) 737-765.

Wili, W. *Horaz und die augusteische Kultur* (Basel 1948).

Wilkinson, L. P. *The Georgics of Virgil* (Cambridge 1969).

Williams, R. D. rev. of Dahlmann, *Der Bienenstaat in Vergils Georgica*, in *CR* n.s. 6 (1956) 170.

Wolff, E. "Das geschichtliche Verstehen in Tacitus Germania", *Hermes* 69 (1934) 121-166.

Woodman, A. J. "Some Implications of *otium* in Catullus 51.13-16", *Latomus* 25 (1966) 217-226.

Wünsch, M. *Lucan-Interpretation* (diss. Kiel 1930).

Wuilleumier, P. "Virgile et le Vieillard de Tarente", *REL* 8 (1930) 325-340.

INDEXES

Index Rerum

umbra, 18
Utopian ethnography, *beatae insulae*, etc., 2, 21-22, 33 n. 86

Varro, 71-72
vates, 25-27

Index Locorum